the Curtain Sketchbook 3

by Wendy Baker

ISBN 978-0-9549758-4-5

Published by Shoestring Book Company
© Copyright by Wendy Baker 2007

Conceived, edited and designed by Wendy Baker

Illustrations by Chrissie Carriere © for Shoestring Book Company

All rights reserved. No part of this work may be reproduced, stored in retrieval system or transmitted in any form or by any means, electronic, electrostatic magnetic tape, mechanical, photocopying, recordings or otherwise without the prior permission in writing to the publisher.

Printed in China by SC International Pte. Ltd

Design by Roseleaf Media

the Curtain Sketchbook 3

Telephone orders: +44 (0) 845 602 1375
email: info@shoestringbooks.co.uk
website: www.shoestringbooks.co.uk

introduction

The CURTAIN SKETCHBOOK 3 is the latest version of the ever popular CURTAIN SKETCHBOOK which I am sure you have come across over the past 25 years as it has become an essential addition to most interior decorators' libraries and used as a quick reference book by curtain makers.

Every 5 years or so I put together an updated version of the CURTAIN SKETCHBOOK as it's important to keep up with the latest interior trends. At present fabrics are fairly bold following in the footsteps of the wallpaper revival. There is an abundance of large floral prints around and ever so wide horizontal striped fabrics everywhere - don't add a large wallpaper print as well or you may have to leave town! Curtain designs tend to be very casual with tied or tab headings and in general they have far less fullness in them, unless you are choosing window treatments for a period house in which case I would use more widths with traditional curtain headings.

As fabrics are pretty expensive nowadays and the making prices seem to have shot up too, I tend to play safe and use fairly plain interesting woven fabrics in natural soft colours adding a wide, deeper toned braid or perhaps a beaded fringe on the leading edge to add a special twist. Try not to end up with a room all in beige/cream/off white as this can often look as though you are living in a bowl of porridge! Use other gentle colours for the sofa and another for the chairs. Long gone are the days of the matching three piece suite. The same goes for dining room chairs, upholster each in a different colour, or use different prints with spots and stripes mixed together.

As usual there is no colour in this book as I leave it up to you to colour the sketches to suit your own décor, or if you are an interior decorator, to suit your client's décor. The sketches which can, of course, be reduced to fit onto a sample board are widely used by Interior Design Colleges in degree courses as well as being a great source of inspiration to many decorators worldwide.

I hope you find this latest sketchbook helpful. Do look on my website at my other sketchbooks which you may also find useful.

contents

Introduction 4
Contents 5
Basic window shapes 6
Measuring up 8
Fabric quantities 9
Basic headings 10

Valances 14
Pelmets 17
Wooden pelmets 19
Tie backs 20
Holdbacks 23
Basic poles and finials ... 24
Modern tracking 26

Curtains/drapes on poles 28
Curtains/drapes
with valances 46
Swags and tails 54
Formal curtains/drapes 64
Curtains/drapes
with pelmets 72
Simply modern 78

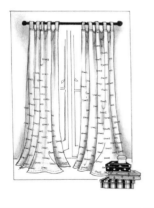

Bay windows 90
Italian stringing 100
Dressed curtains 106
Covered laths 113
Alcoves 116
Portieres 122

Appliquéd
curtains/drapes 126
Bedroom curtains 130
Voile/sheers 138
Kitchen curtain/blinds ... 146
Difficult windows 152
Alternative
window coverings 155

Café/short/doors 159
Lambrequins 161
Blinds/shades 162
Tablecovers 164
Headboards 165
Cushions 167

basic windows

BASIC WINDOW

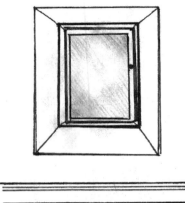

RECESSED WINDOW

DOUBLE COTTAGE WINDOW

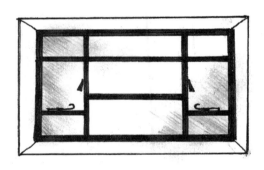

1930's METAL FRAME

GEORGIAN SASH

ARCHED GEORGIAN SASH

basic doors

Half Glazed Door

Single Patio Doors

French Doors With Side Windows

French Doors In Bay

measuring up

Make sure you use a metal retractable measure to avoid making mistakes at this point accurate measuring is vital. Decisions have to be made before you measure, such as whether you are having a pole, tracking concealed by a covered lath, a pelmet or a simple blind.
To measure accurately you should have the pole or whichever type of curtain tracking in position in order to measure the drop (length) of the curtain correctly. Generally these are fixed about 20cms (8 ins) above the architrave, but this does vary greatly depending on the position of the window to the ceiling. Wooden poles should be 6.3 cms (2ins) in diameter if the curtains are long and can be as thin as 2.5 (1ins) for voile (sheers) curtains or short ones.

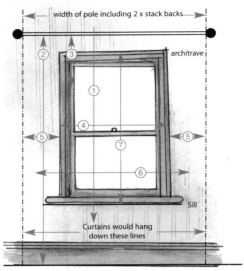

BASIC WINDOW

MEASURING CUT LENGTH CURTAINS
For short curtains, measure from the pole or tracking to 13cms (5ins) below sill (1)
For long curtains measure from the pole or tracking to the floor (2) add extra if you want the curtains to break on the floor. Pelmets or valances fix the pelmet board at the same height as you would a pole. The length of the pelmet or valance should, as a rough guide, be 1/6 of the total length of the curtains, so divide the length of the curtains by 6 to find the correct length (3). Finally add 1.3 (5ins) to allow for your heading and hem.

MEASURING CURTAIN WIDTH
Measure between the architraves (4) and add on an extra 30cms (12 ins) on each side to allow for stack backs (5). Remember to add seam allowances.

MEASURING UP FOR BLINDS
Fix blinds approximately 20cms (8ins) above the architrave to allow as much light as possible into the room. Measure the width between the architraves and add 5cms (2in) each side (6). To work out the length, measure the length of the window and add 20cms (8in) above the architrave plus 3 cm (1in) below the sill (7).

MEASURING UP FOR CURTAINS AND BLINDS IN A RECESS
Measure the length from the top to the bottom of the recess. Measure the width of the recess. If you choose blinds, always remember to check the measurements at the top, middle and bottom as windows can be irregular. If the window is very small, it is preferable to hang curtains outside the recess to avoid losing too much light.

MEASURING UP FOR SWAGS AND TAILS...
For the swag length, measure the width of the pelmet board that is going to carry your tracking and add approximately 40cm (16in). To calculate the swag depth, multiply the required length by 2. The inner edge of the tail should be the same length as the swag. The outer edge should be about three-quarters of the total curtain length.

CALCULATING FABRIC REQUIREMENTS
Divide the curtain width by the width of your fabric to find the number of curtain drops (lengths) required. Decide on the fullness you require. Traditional Curtains should have 2-3 widths of fabric, unless the fabric is very thick, and the more contemporary styles are generally about 2 widths of fullness. Obviously curtain panels have no fullness at all. Multiply the number of drops by the cut length measurement to find the required amount of fabric. If your fabric has a pattern, allow one pattern repeat extra for each drop.

fabric quantities

Curtains/Drapes
2 ½ Heading Fullness
30cm heading and hem allowance, 2 x 7cm overlaps and 2 x 8cm returns
Measurements in metres

Length of track or pole up to:

120 cm fabric	0.55	1.00	1.50	1.95	2.45	2..90	3.35	3.85	4.30
137cm fabric	0.70	1.20	1.75	2.30	2.85	3.35	3.90	4.45	5.00
150cm fabric	0.80	1.40	2.00	2.55	3.15	3.75	4.35	4.90	5.50
No. of widths	2	3	4	5	6	7	8	9	10

Finished Length

1.80	4.20	6.30	8.40	10.50	12.60	14.70	16.80	18.90	21.00
1.90	4.40	6.60	8.80	11.00	13.20	15.40	17.60	19.80	22.00
2.00	4.60	6.90	9.20	11.50	13.80	16.10	18.40	20.70	23.00
2.10	4.80	7.20	9.60	12.00	14.40	16.80	19.20	21.60	24.00
2.20	5.00	7.50	10.00	12.50	15.00	17.50	20.00	22.50	25.00
2.30	5.20	7.80	10.40	13.00	15.60	18.20	20.80	23.40	26.00
2.40	5.40	8.10	10.80	13.50	16.20	18.90	21.60	24.30	27.00
2.50	5.60	8.40	11.20	14.00	16.80	19.60	22.40	25.20	28.00
2.60	5.80	8.70	11.60	14.50	17.40	20.30	23.20	26.10	29.00
2.70	6.00	9.00	12.00	15.00	18.00	21.00	24.00	27.00	30.00
2.80	6.20	9.30	12.40	15.50	18.60	21.70	24.80	27.90	31.00
2.90	6.40	9.60	12.80	16.00	19.20	22.40	25.60	28.80	32.00
3.00	6.60	9.90	13.20	16.50	19.80	23.10	26.40	29.70	33.00
3.10	6.80	10.20	13.60	17.00	20.40	23.80	27.20	30.60	34.00
3.20	7.00	10.50	14.00	17.50	21.00	24.50	28.00	31.50	35.00
3.30	7.20	10.80	14.40	18.00	21.60	25.20	28.80	32.40	36.00
3.40	7.40	11.10	14.80	18.50	22.20	25.90	29.60	33.30	37.00
3.50	7.60	11.40	15.20	19.00	22.80	26.60	30.40	34.20	38.00

We wish to thank Merrick & Day for allowing us to use these calculations from The Fabric Quantity Handbook.

basic curtain headings

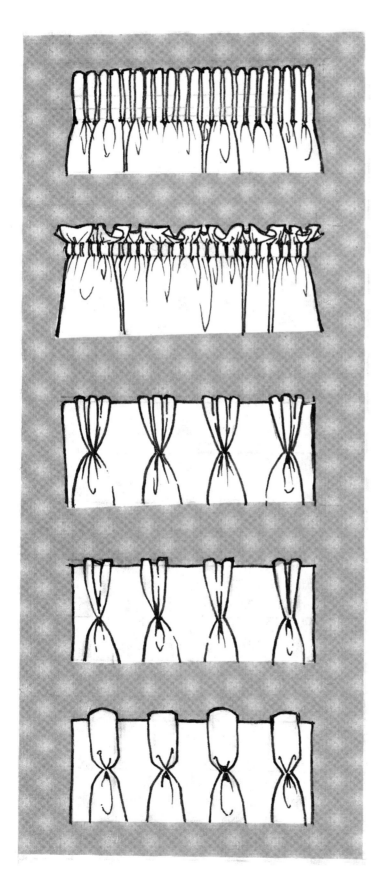

1. Pencil Pleat

2. Unstructured

3. Triple Pinch Pleat

4. Double Pinch Pleat

5. Goblet or Tulip

basic curtain headings

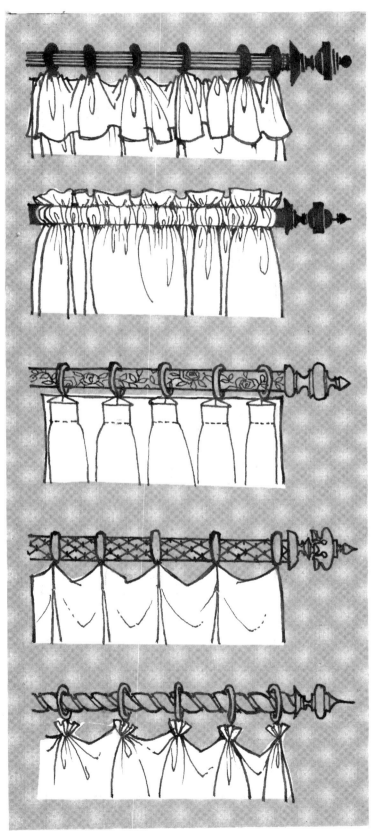

6. Floppy Heading – Narrow Tape

7. Slotted Heading With Stand Up

8. Narrow Soft Box Pleated – No Tape

9. Soft Inverted Pinch Pleats – No Tape

10. Tiny Soft Pinch Pleats – No Tape

basic curtain headings

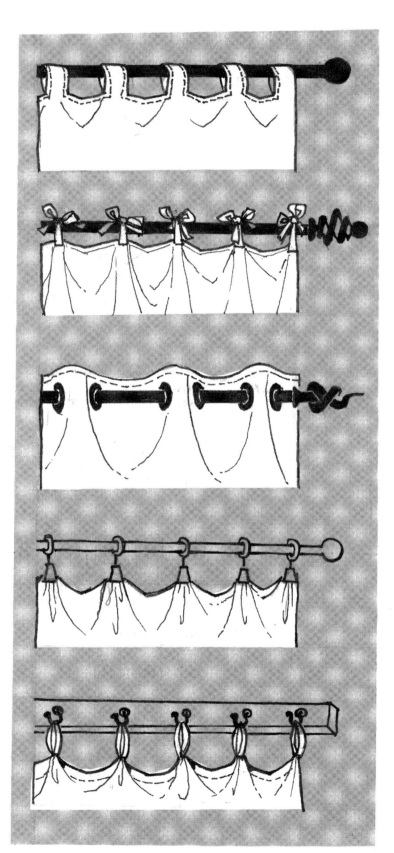

1. Tab
2. Ties
3. Eyelet
4. Clip
5. Loops

basic valances

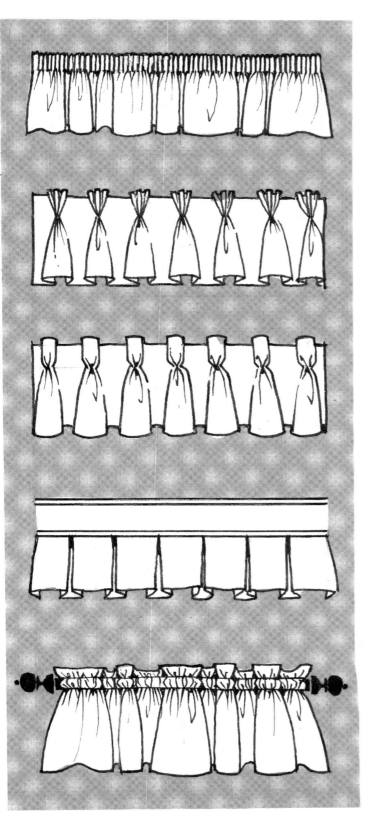

1. Pencil Pleated Neading
2. Pinch Pleated Neading
3. Goblet Neading
4. Box Pleated Heading
5. Slotted Heading with Stand Up

valances

1

2

3

4

Valances

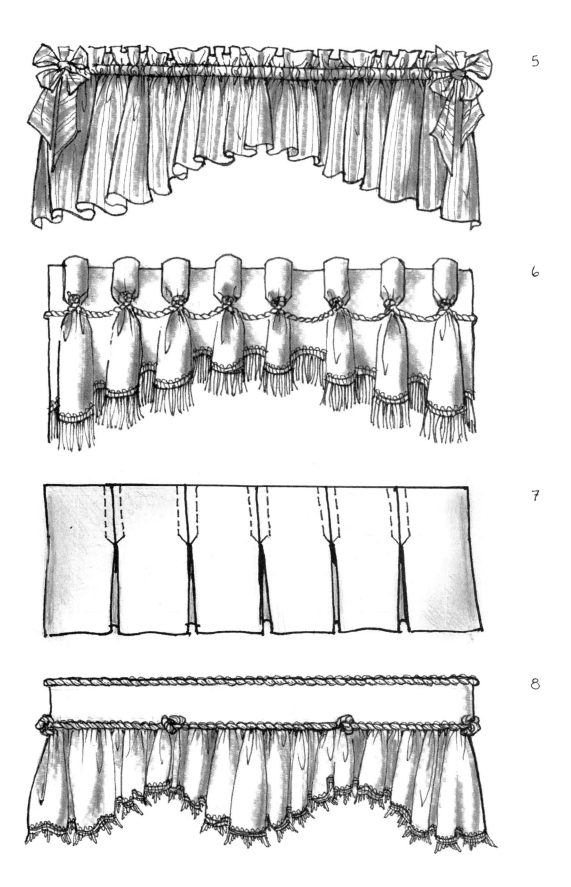

5

6

7

8

valances

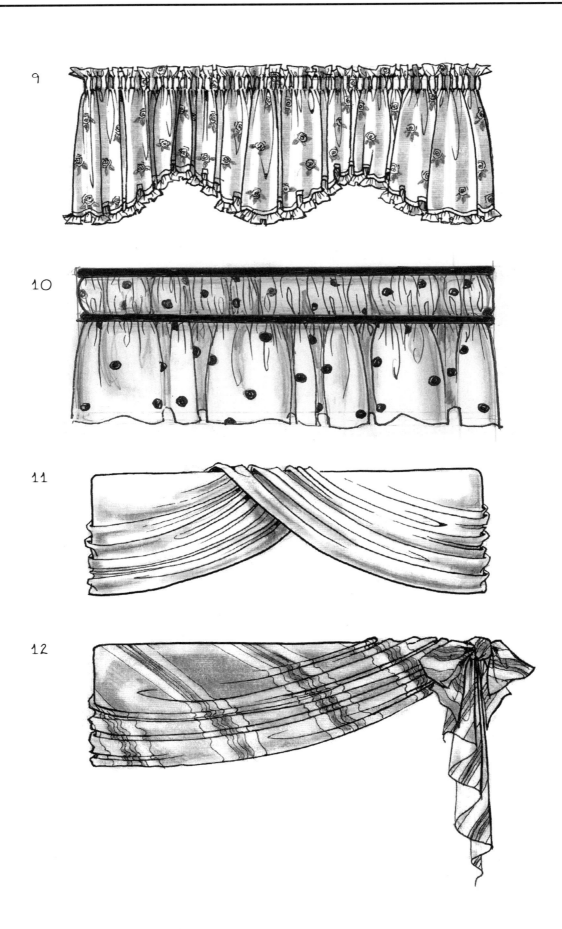

9

10

11

12

pelmets

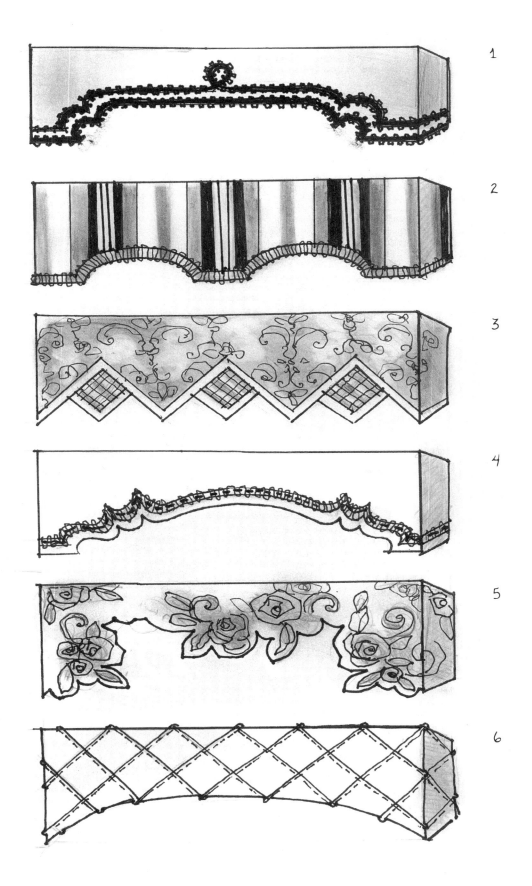

1
2
3
4
5
6

pelmets

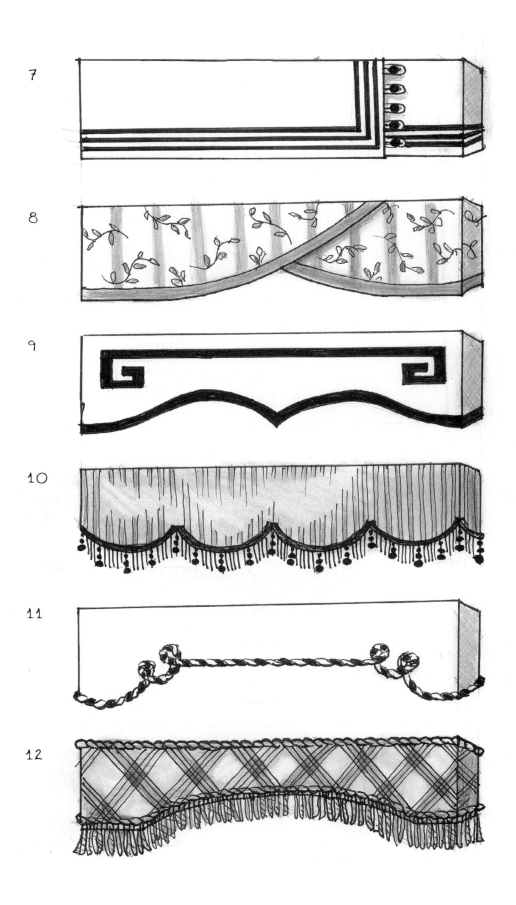

traditional wooden pelmets

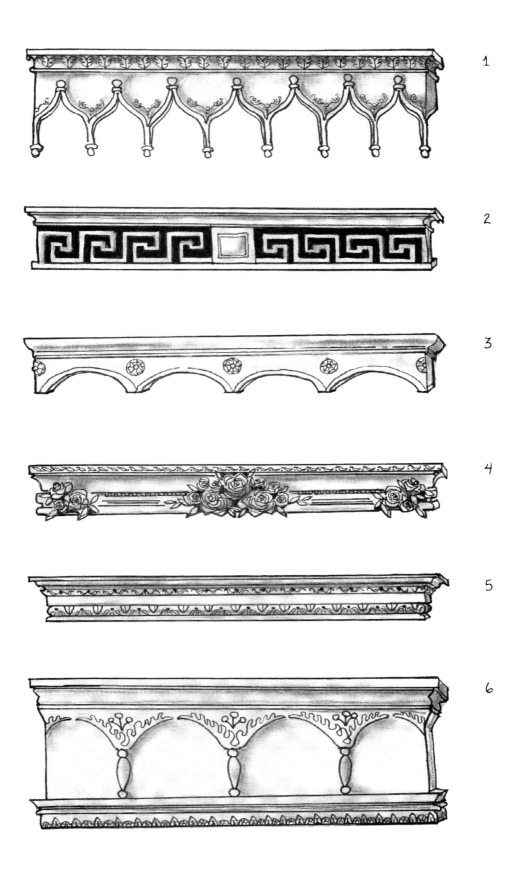

1

2

3

4

5

6

tie backs

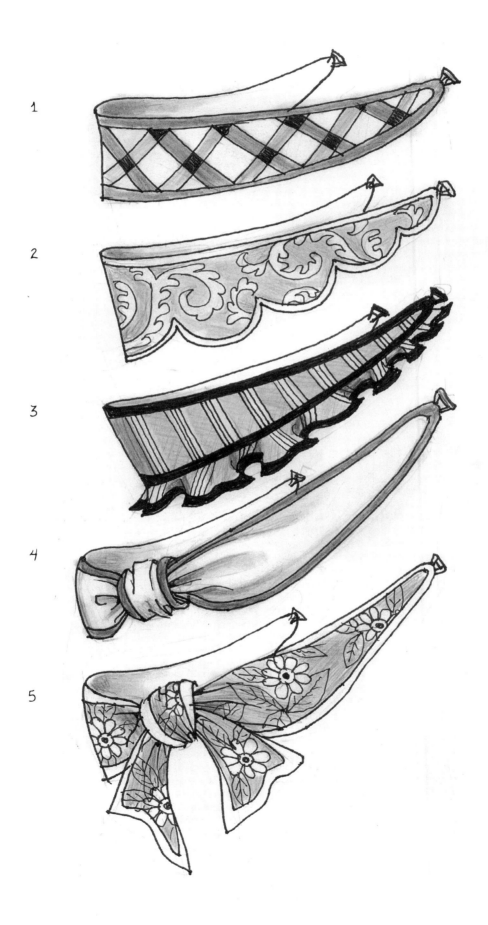

1
2
3
4
5

tie backs

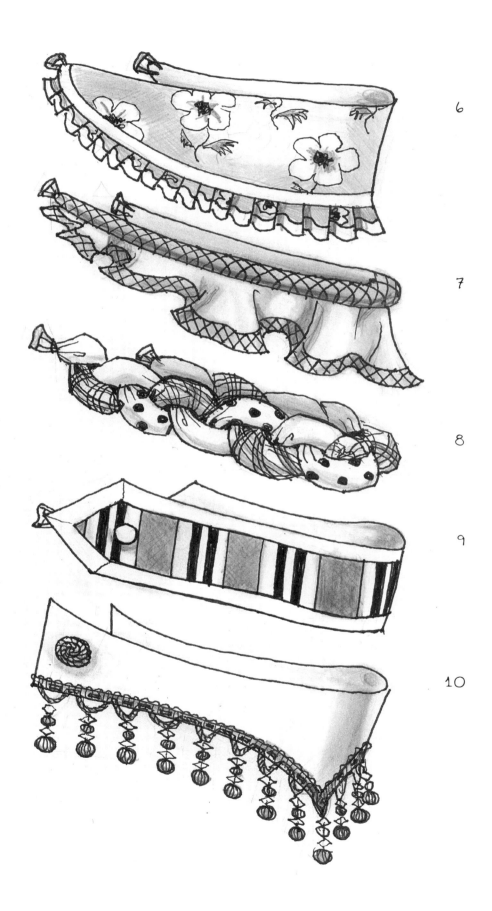

6

7

8

9

10

tie backs

1
2
3
4
5

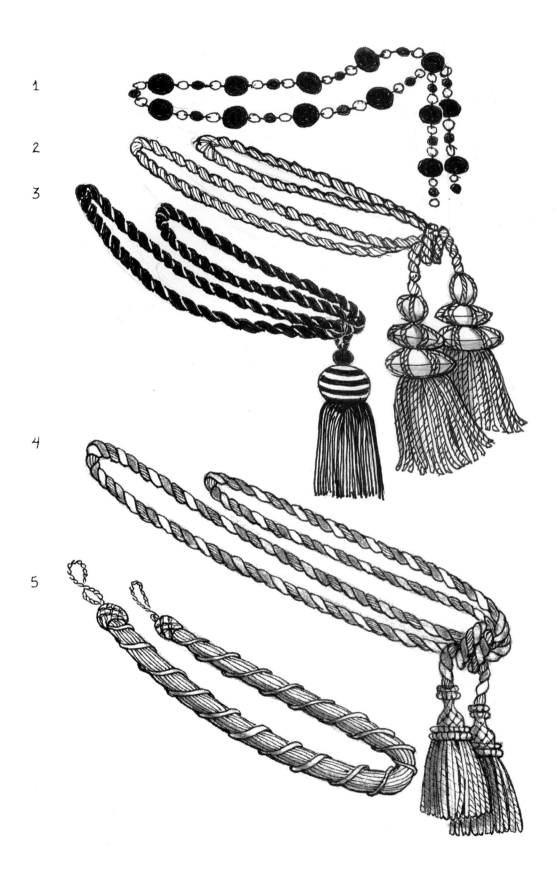

hold backs

1
2
3
4
5
6

poles and finials - traditional

 1. Ball

 2. Provencal style

 3. Reeded ball and pole

 4. Fluted ball

 5. Acorn

 6. Urn - decorative pole

 7. Trumpet - two colours of wood

 8. Art Deco

 9. Banded ball - fabric covered pole

 10. Inverted rib and ogee

 11. Style of early Victorian 'Spinning Top'

 12. Leaf and acorn

 13. Minaret - candy twist pole

 14. Victorian scroll

 15. Coronet - decorative pole

 16. Otterman

poles and finials - modern

 1. Steel spire

 9. Roped ball

 2. Wooden bamboo ball

 10. Roped cone

 3. Steel ribbon ball

 11. Steel trumpet

 4. Iron button

 12. Steel corkscrew

 5. Iron ball

 13. Steel rib

 6. Iron knot

 14. Metal ball

 7. Cage and ball

 15. Steel spotted ball

 8. Shepherd's crook

 16. Three tone cone balls

modern tracking - tension wires

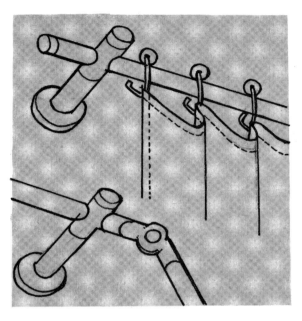

1. Stainless steel roller-line pole - can also be used for angles

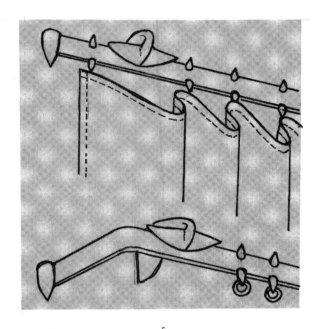

2. Stainless steel flat pole - curves for a bay window

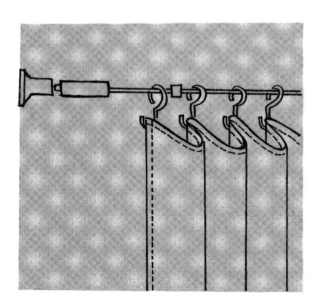

3. Tension wire system used from wall to wall

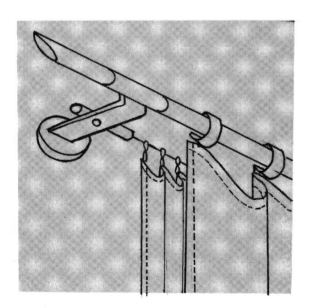

4. Stainless steel pole - can be used with tension wire for second pole

panel glide system

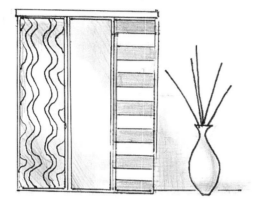

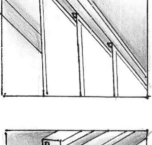

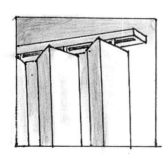

Panel Glide...

A system that brings a totally new dimension to a room.
Hand cord or electronically operated.

Hand operated version uses an aluminium drawrod. When panels are connected the leading panel will cause all the others to follow in sequence.

Hand operated systems are available up to 6M wide. Maximum length for electronically operated system is 10metres.

Panel fold....

A motorised system which can be operated by a fixed wall switch or remote control. Suitable for applications up to 5m wide and 3m drop

curtains on poles

curtains on poles

curtains on poles

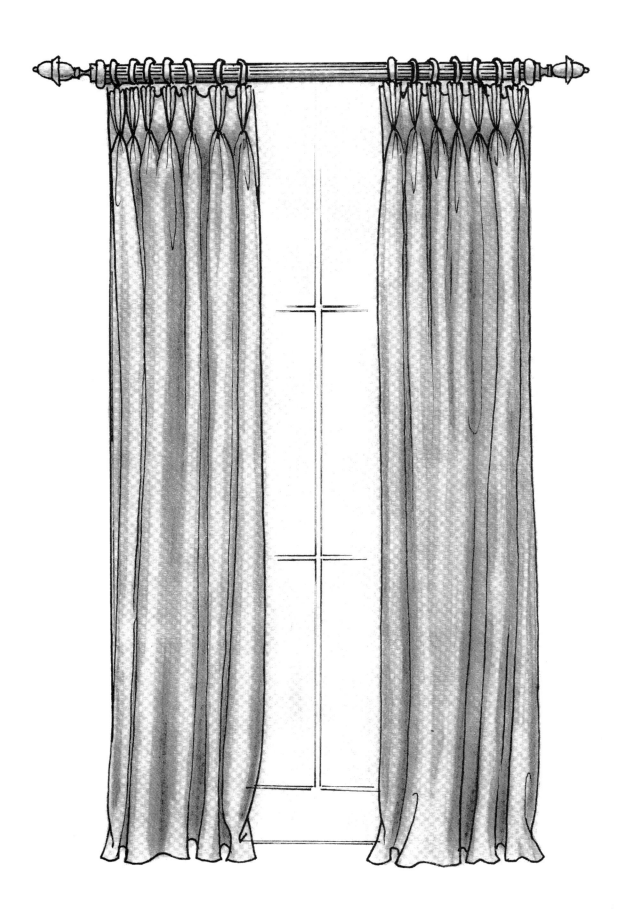

curtains on poles

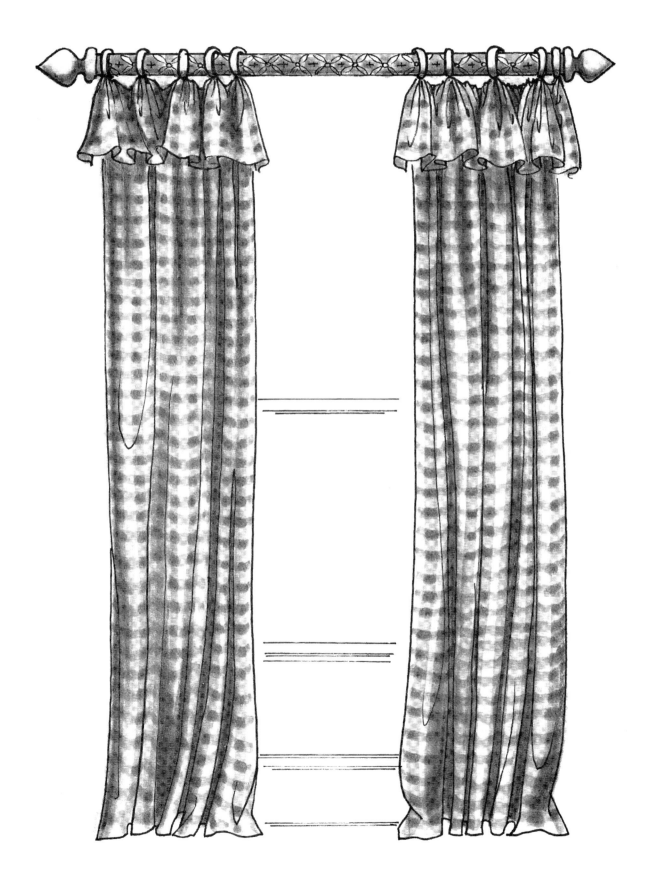

curtains on poles

curtains on poles

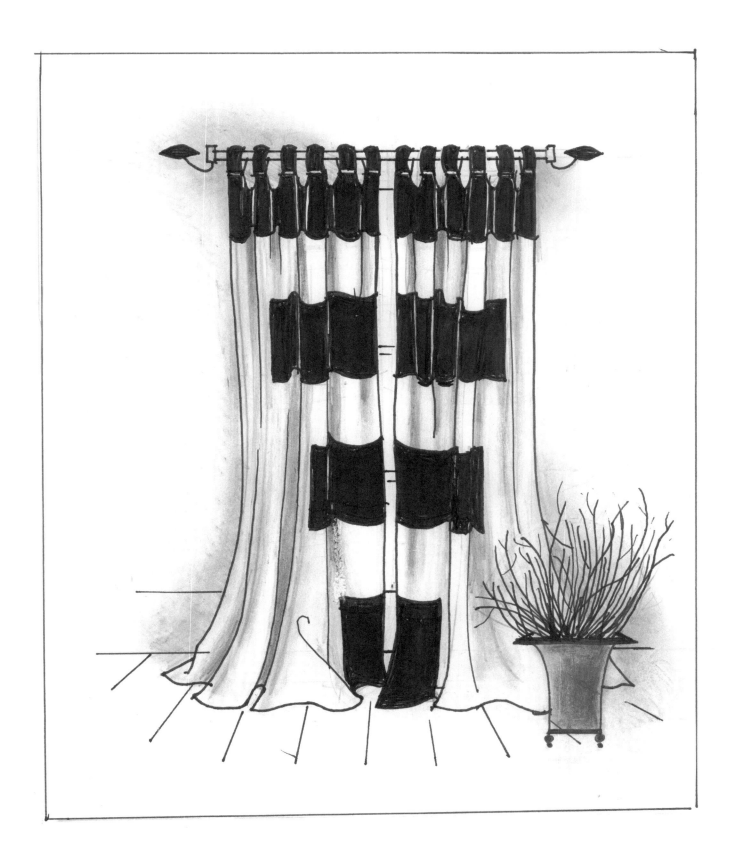

curtains on poles

curtains on poles

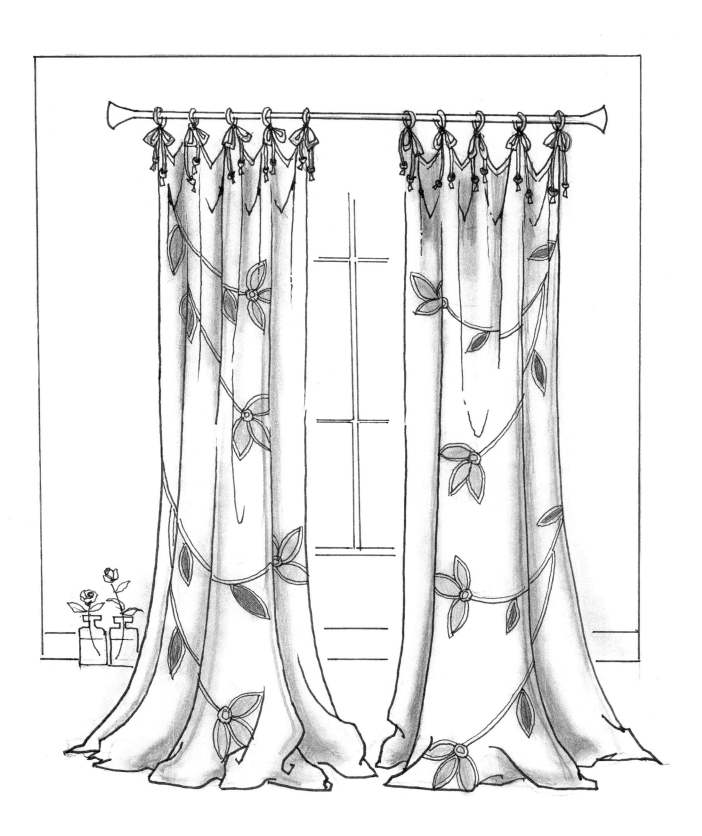

curtains on poles

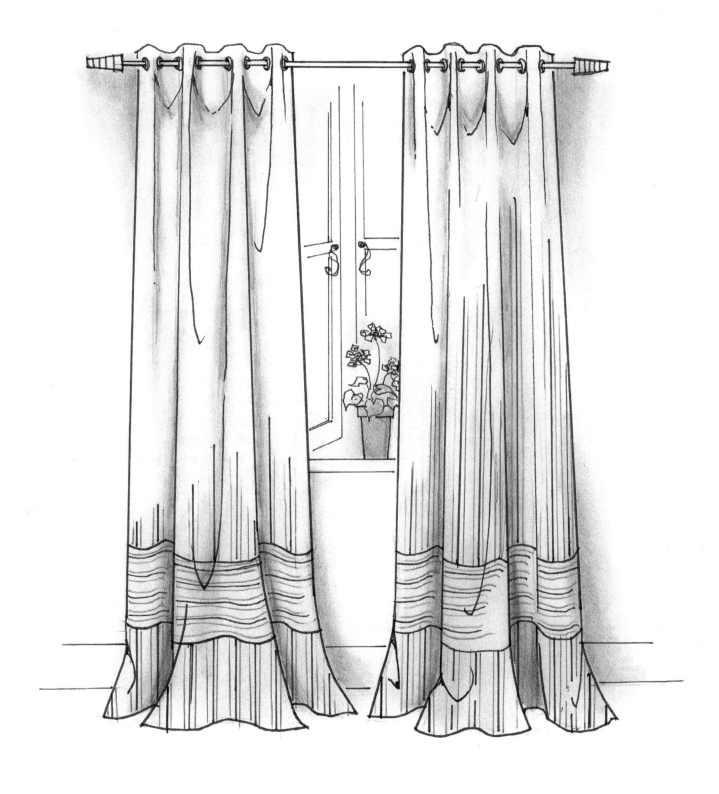

curtains on poles

curtains on poles

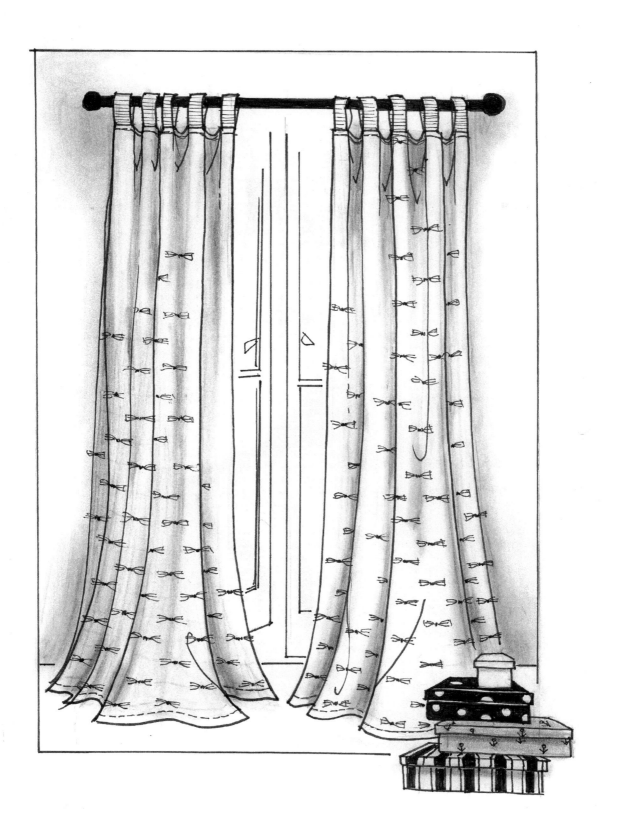

curtains on poles

curtains on poles

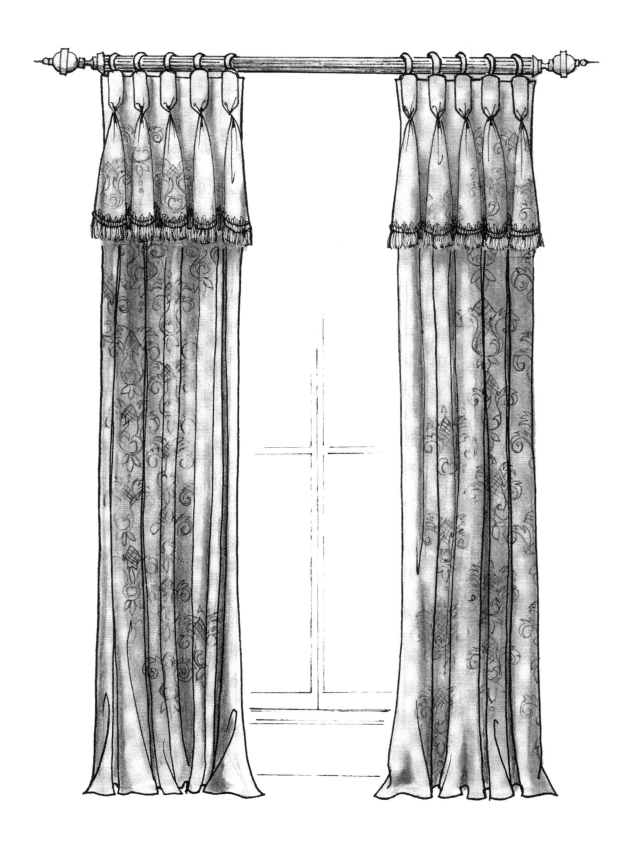

curtains on poles

curtains on poles

curtains on poles

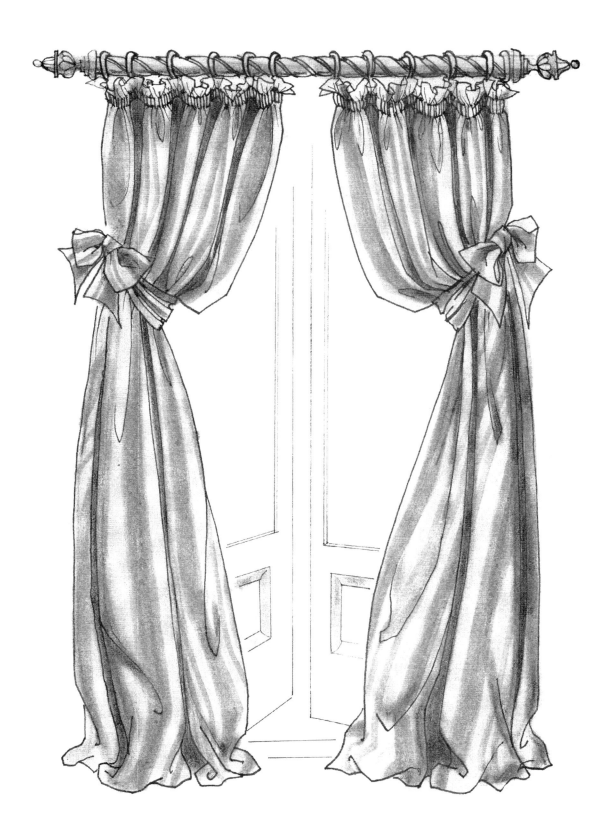

curtains on poles

curtains on poles

curtains with valances

curtains with valances

curtains with valances

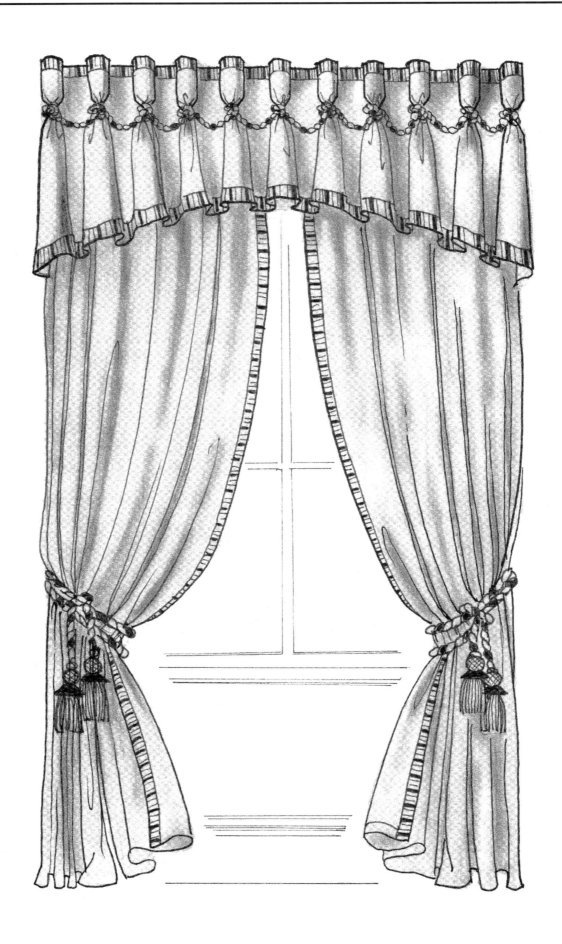

curtains with valances

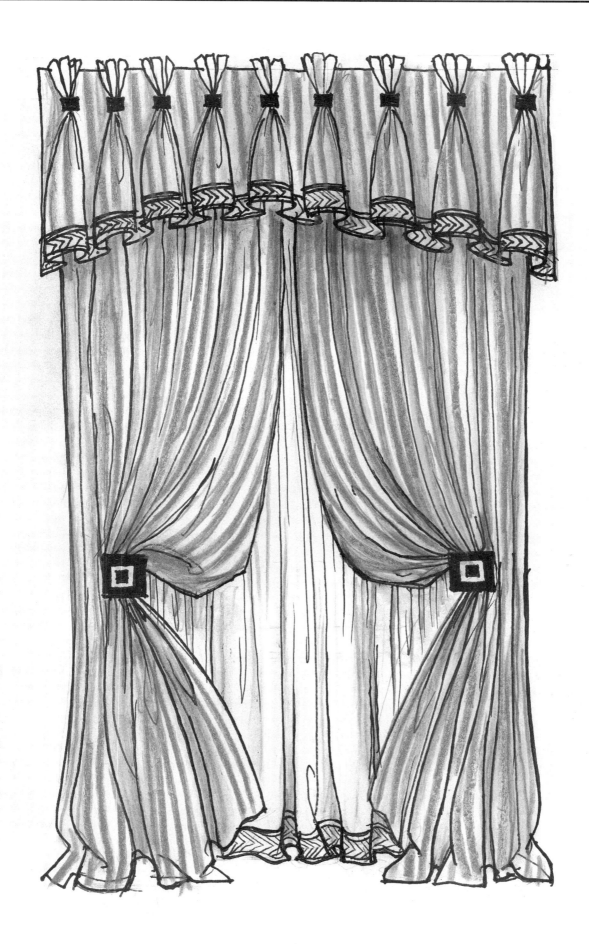

curtains with valances

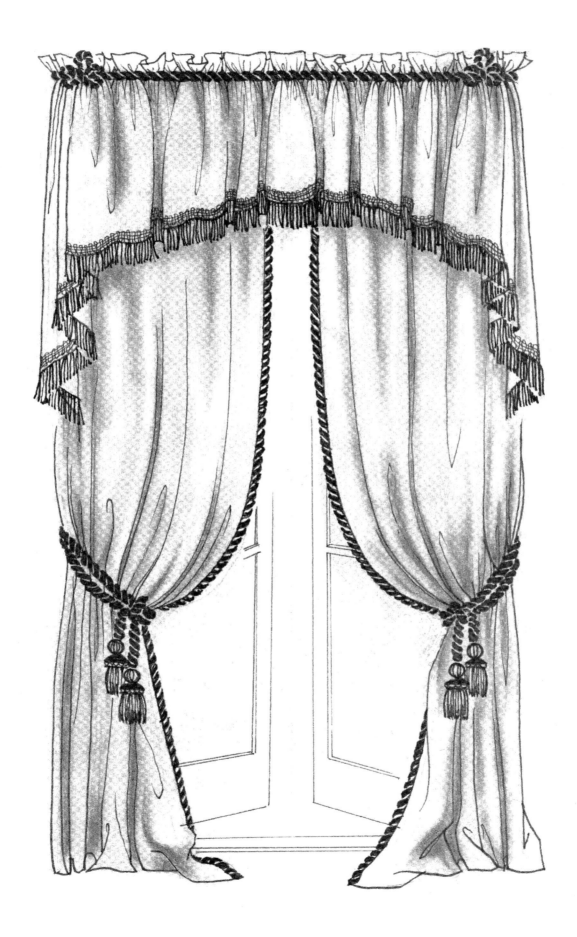

curtains with valances

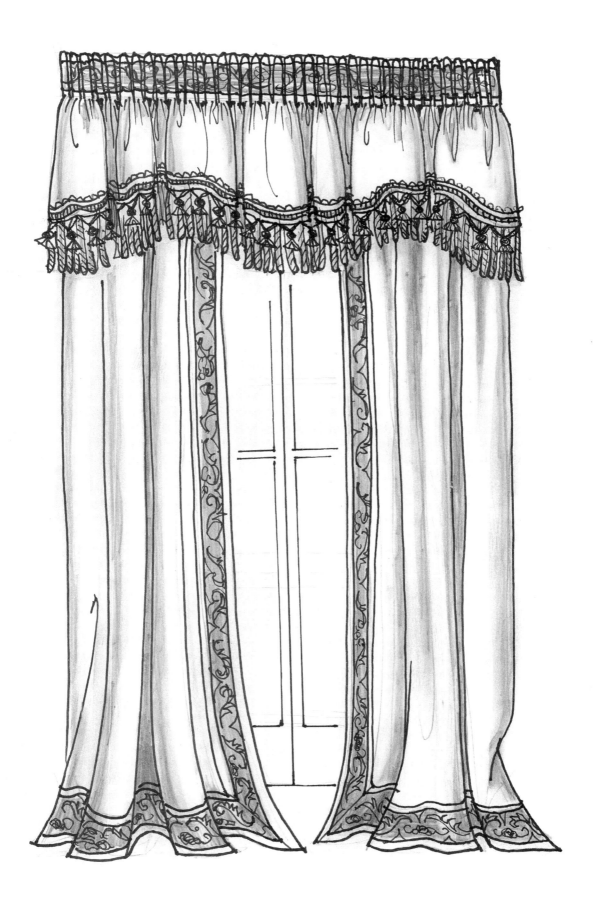

curtains with valances

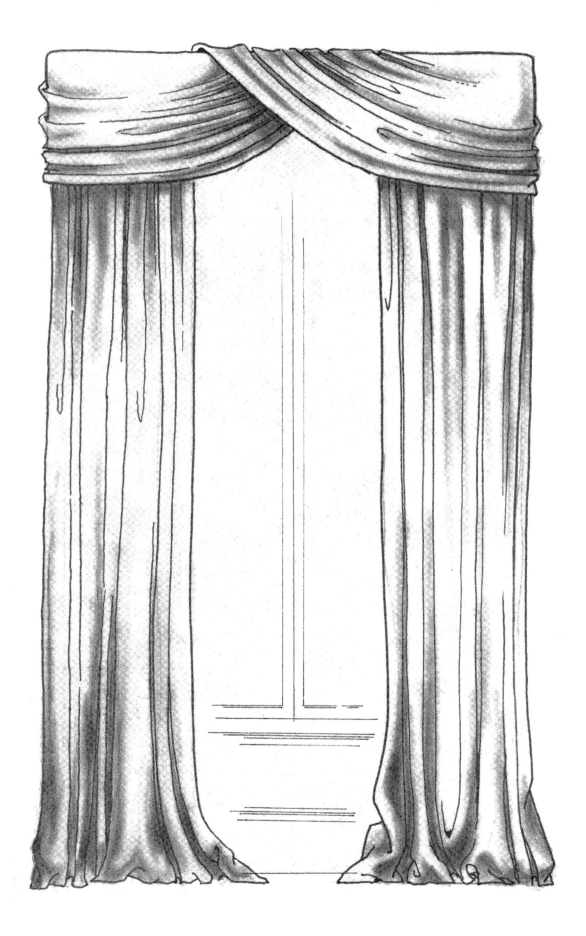

curtains with valances

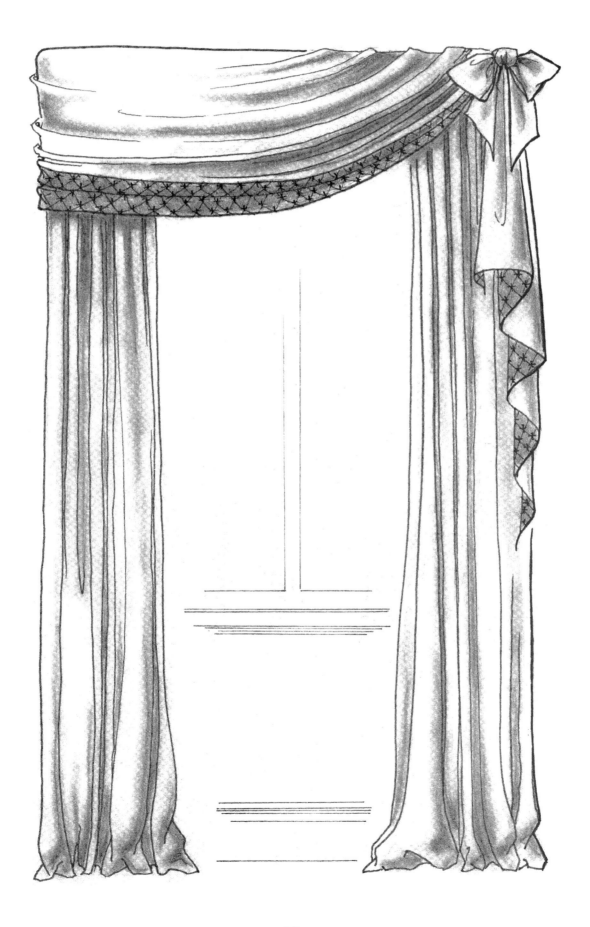

swags and tails

swags and tails

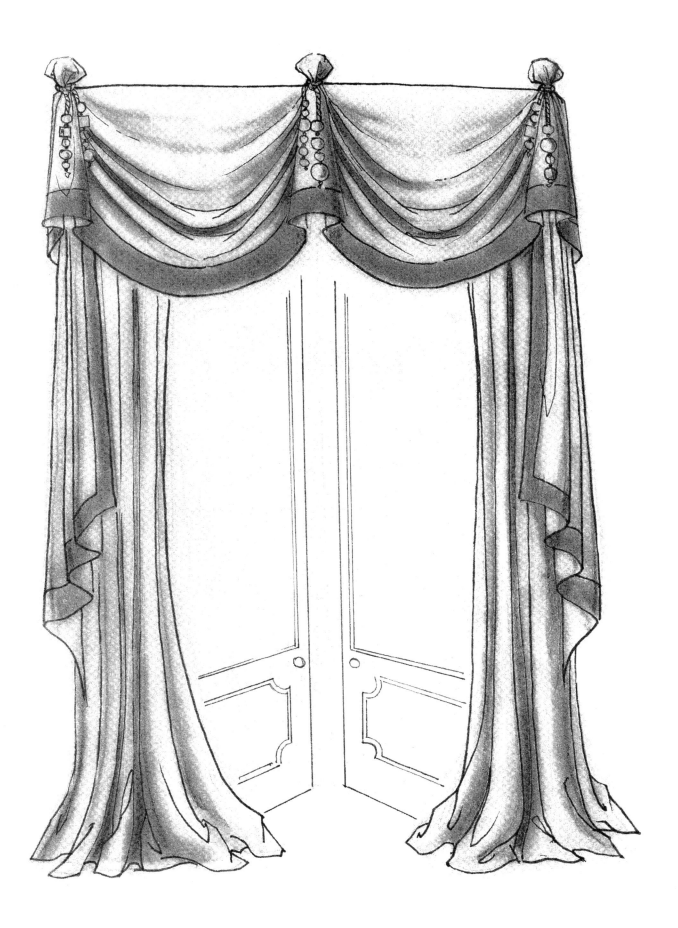

swags and tails

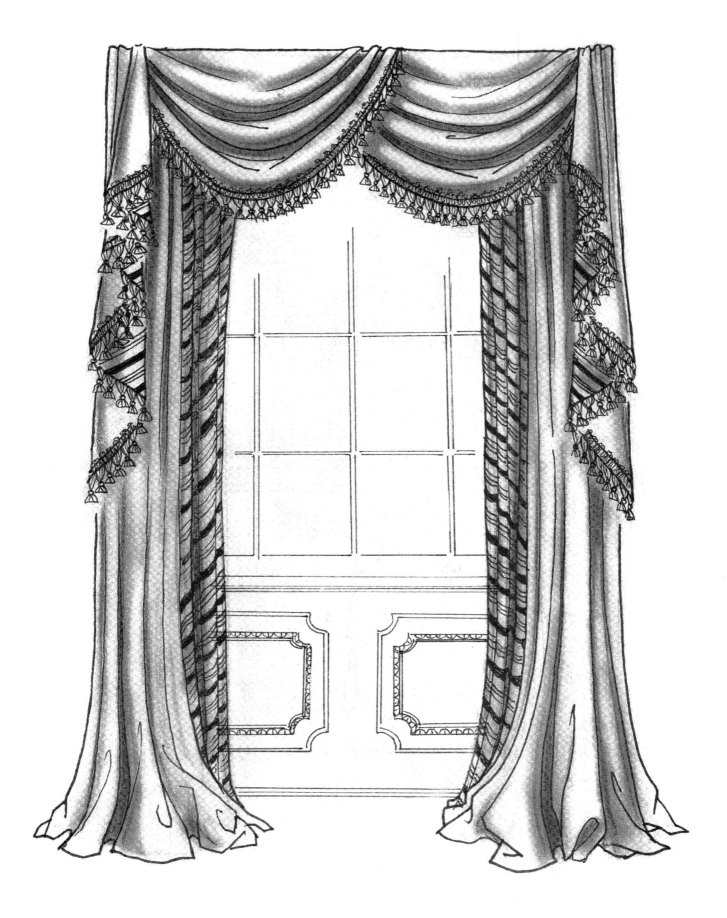

swags and tails

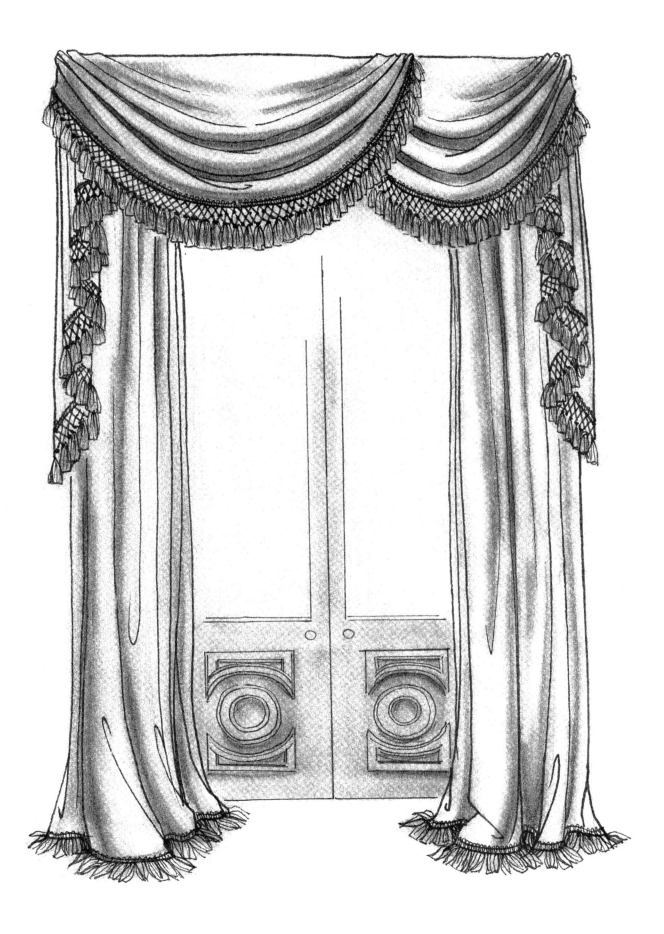

swags and tails

swags and tails

swags and tails

swags and tails

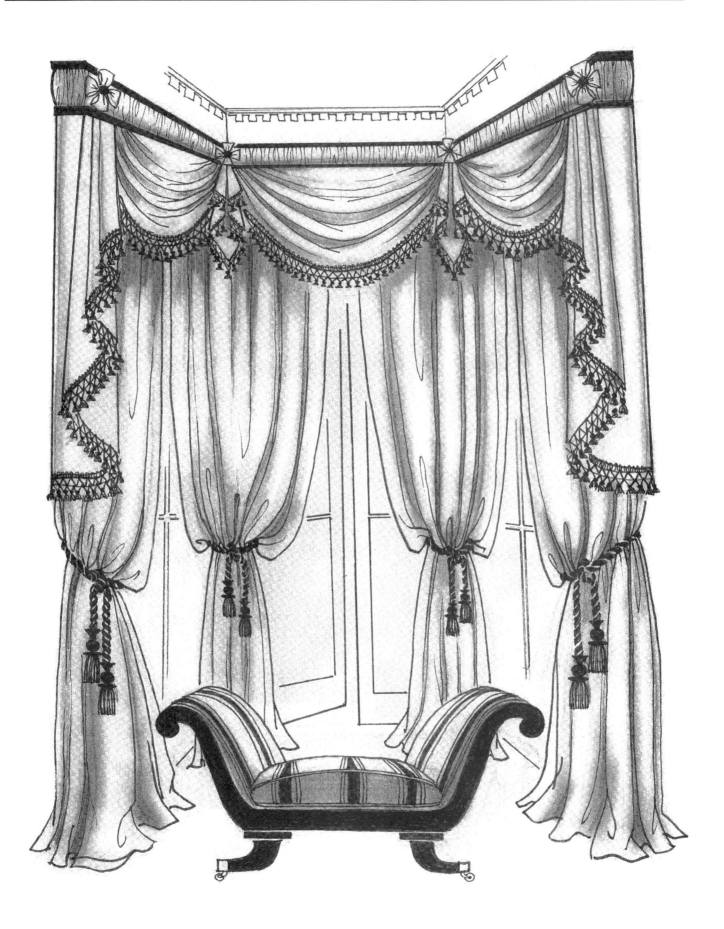

formal curtains

formal curtains

formal curtains

formal curtains

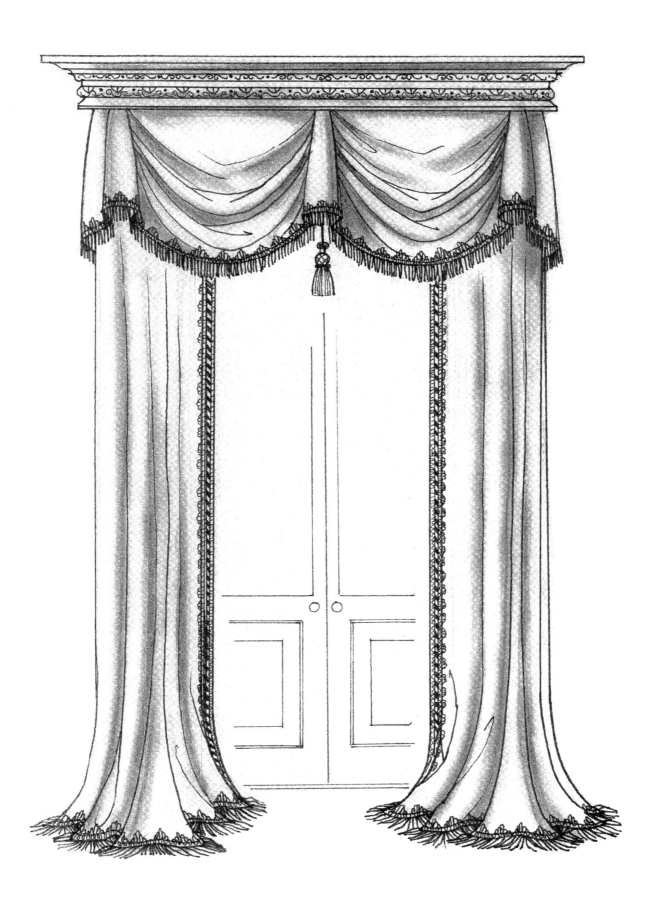

formal curtains

formal curtains

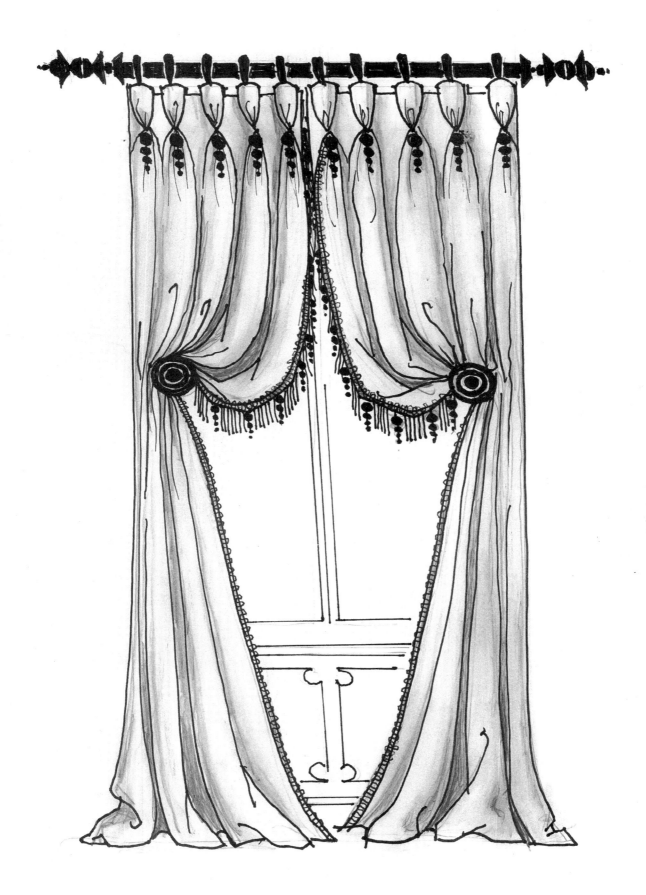

formal curtains

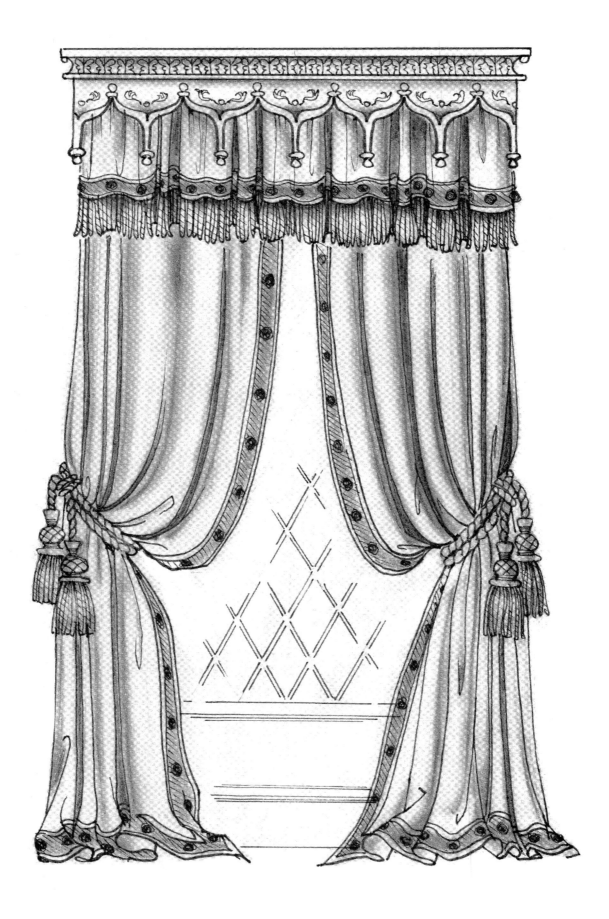

formal curtains

formal curtains

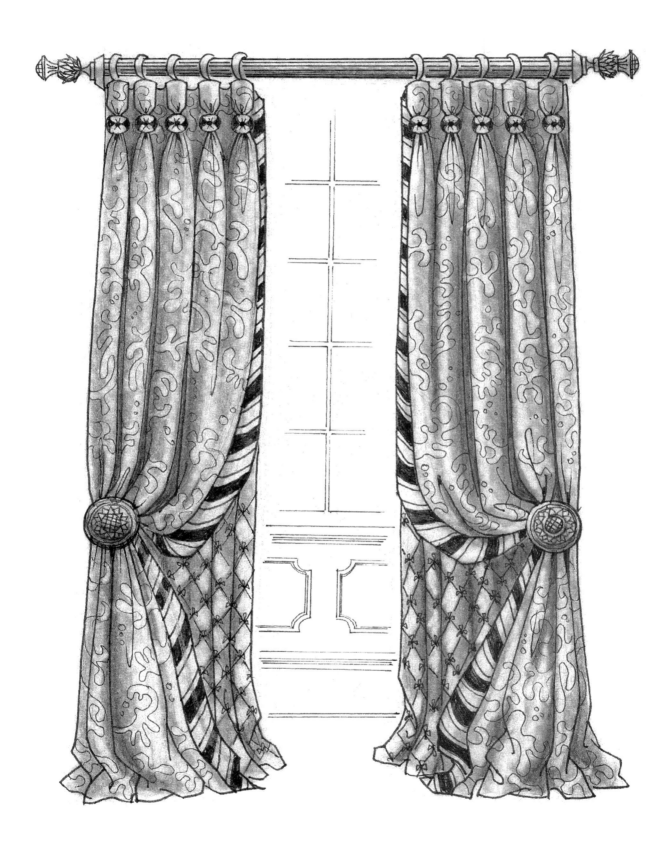

formal curtains

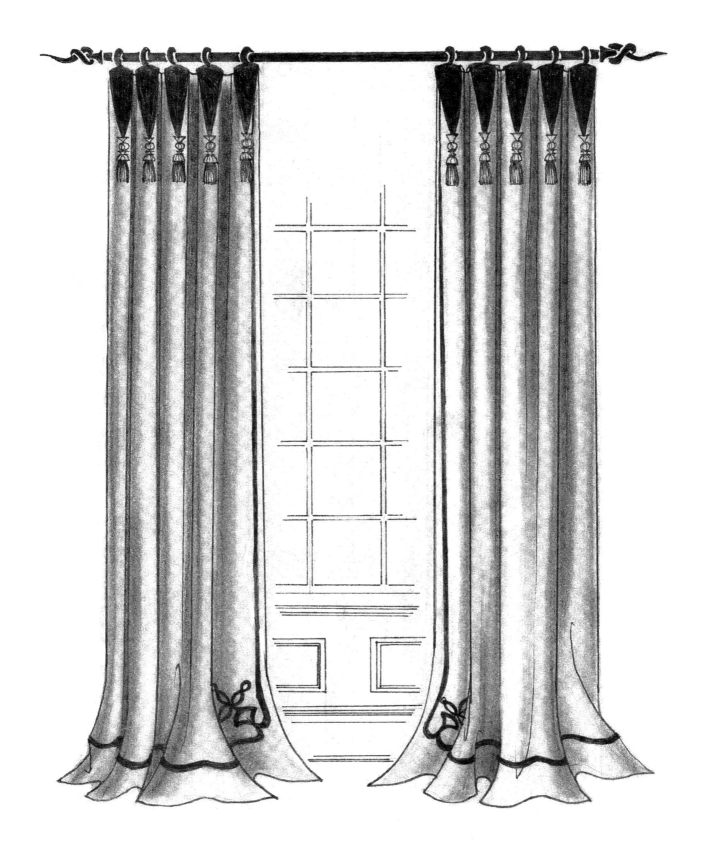

curtains with pelmets

curtains with pelmets

curtains with pelmets

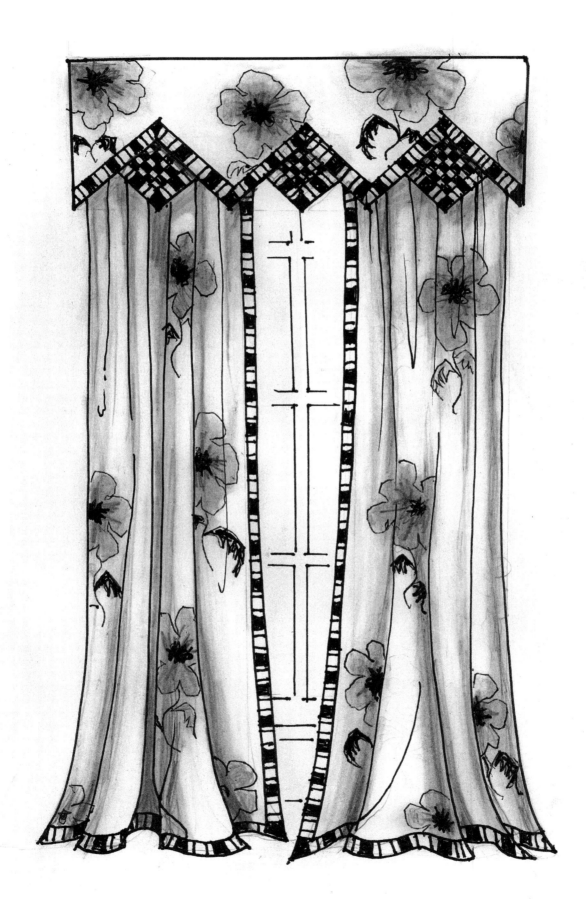

curtains with pelmets

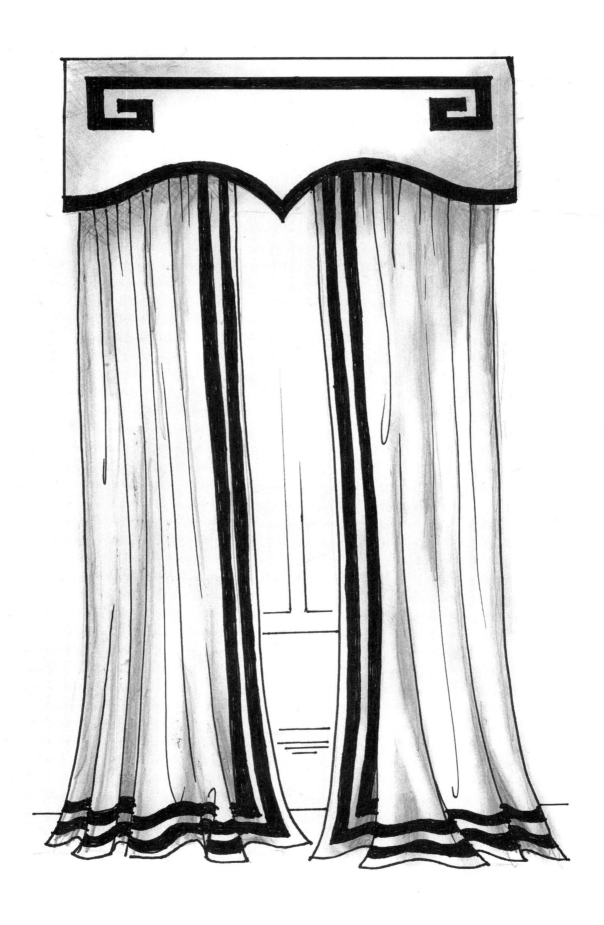

curtains with pelmets

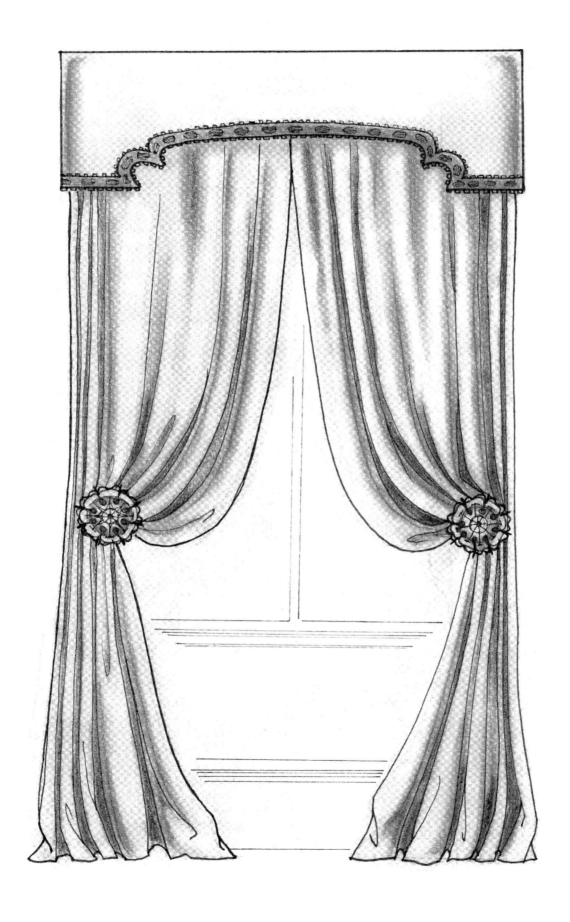

curtains with pelmets

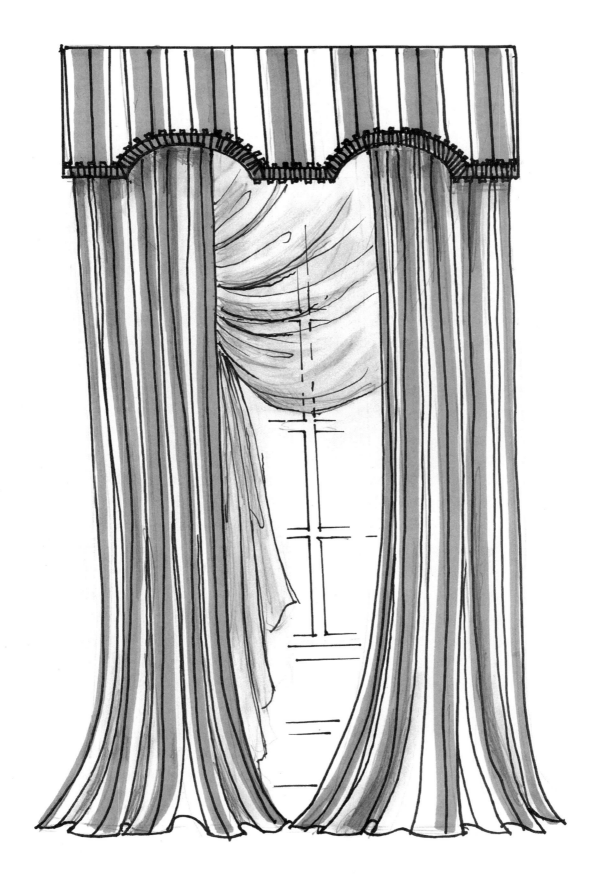

simply modern

simply modern

simply modern

simply modern

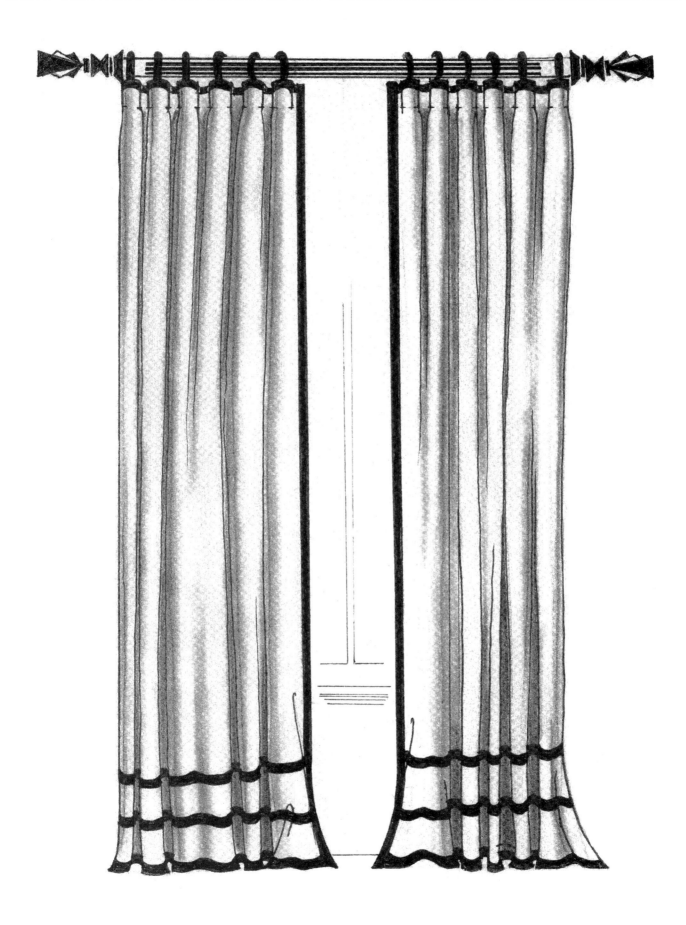

simply modern

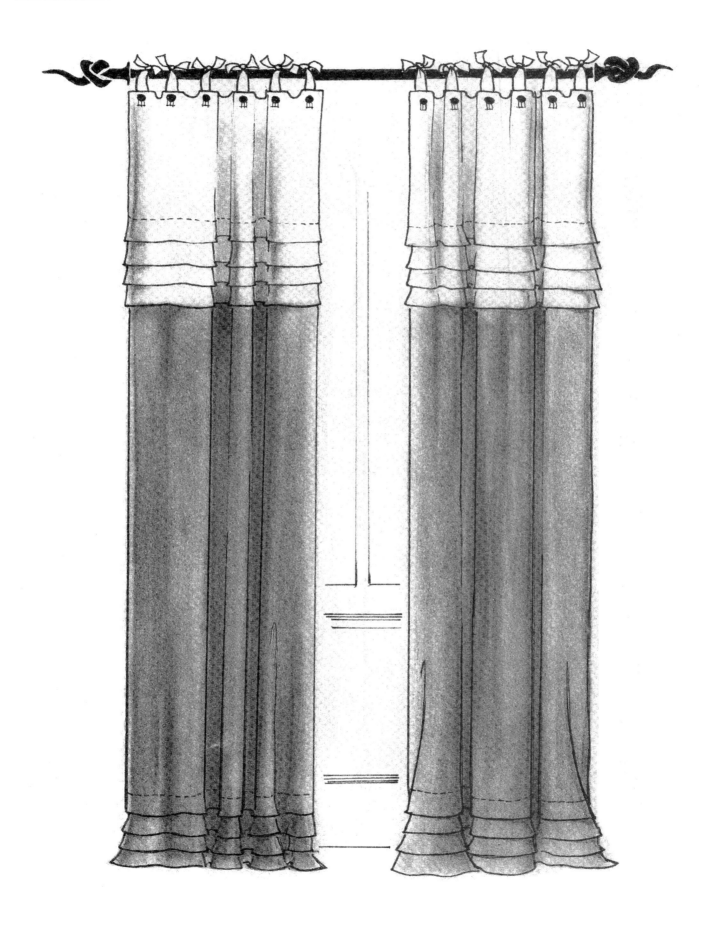

simply modern

simply modern

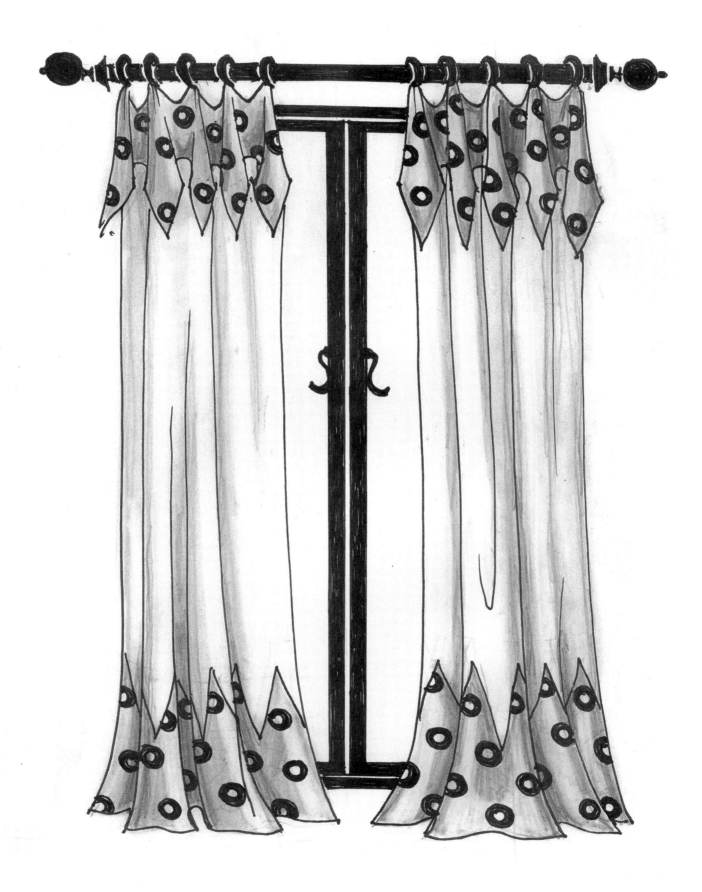

simply modern

simply modern

simply modern

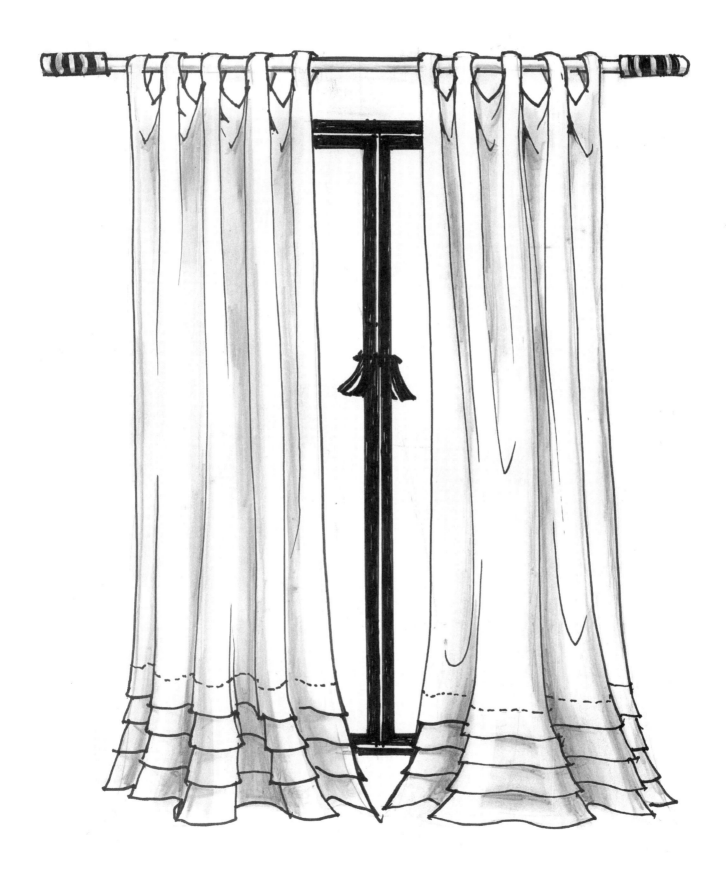

simply modern

simply modern

bay windows

bay windows

bay windows

bay windows

bay windows

bay windows

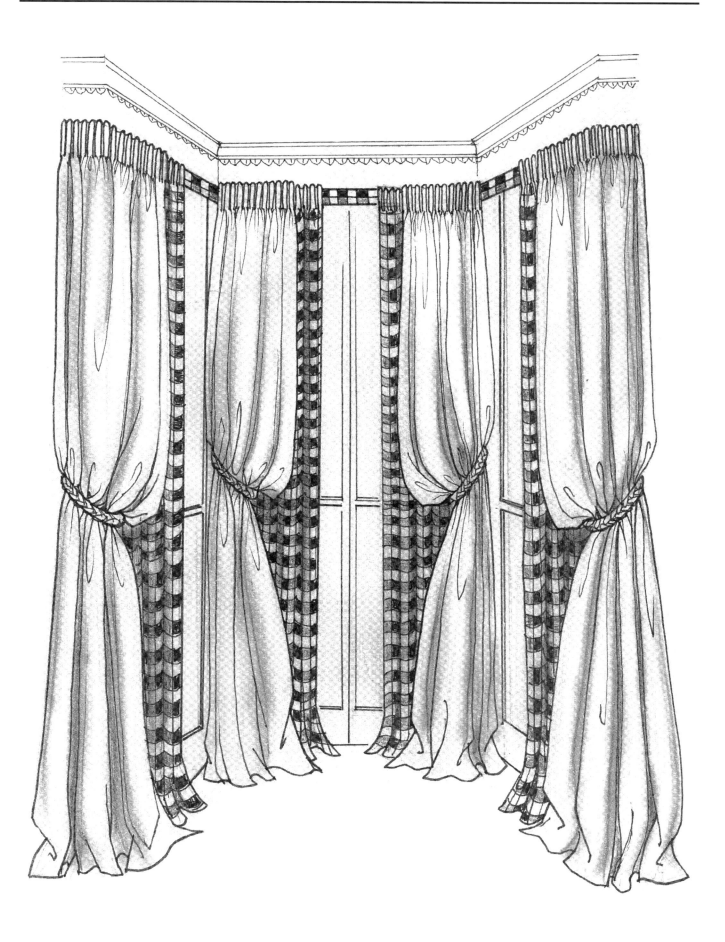

bay windows

bay windows

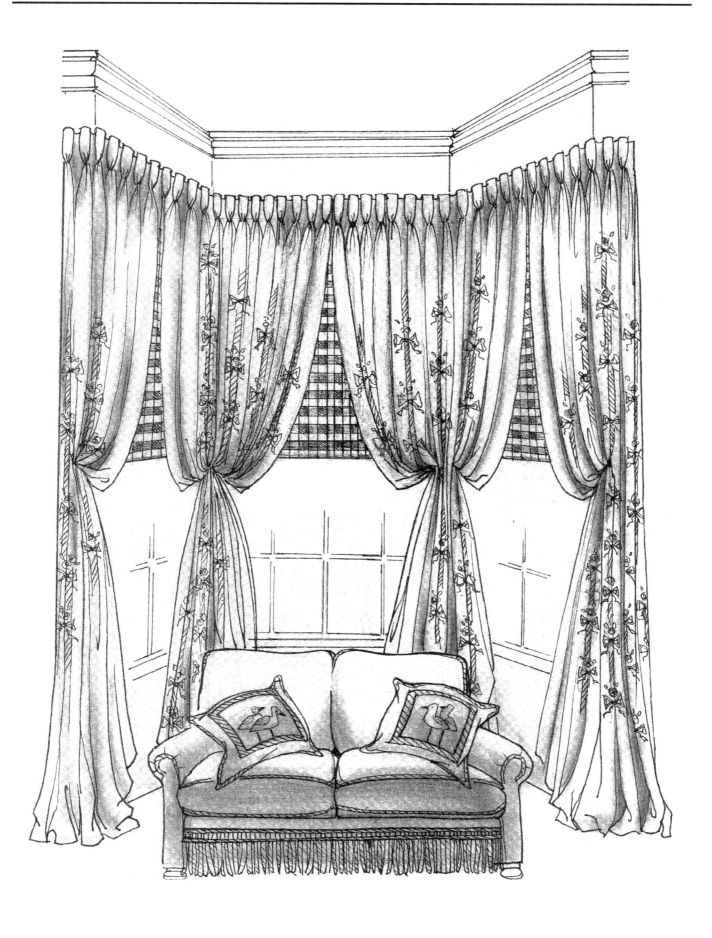

bay windows

bay windows

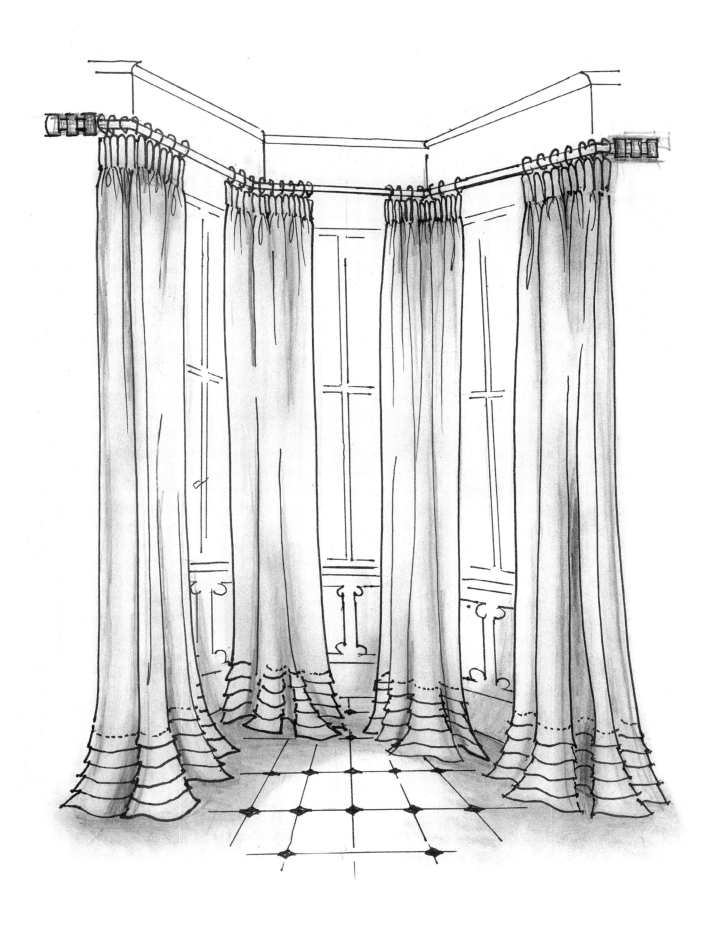

Italian stringing

Italian stringing

Italian stringing

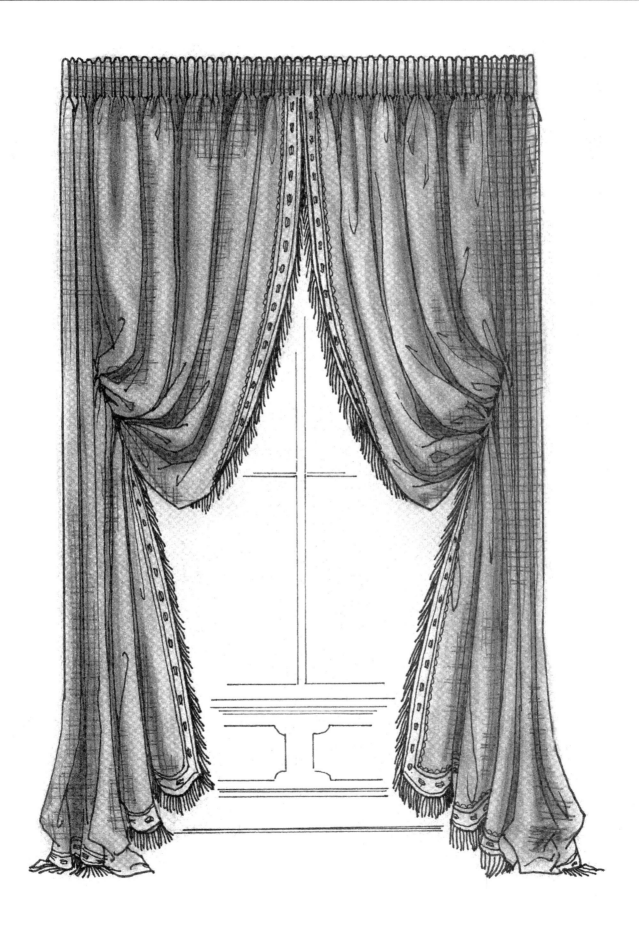

Italian stringing

Italian stringing

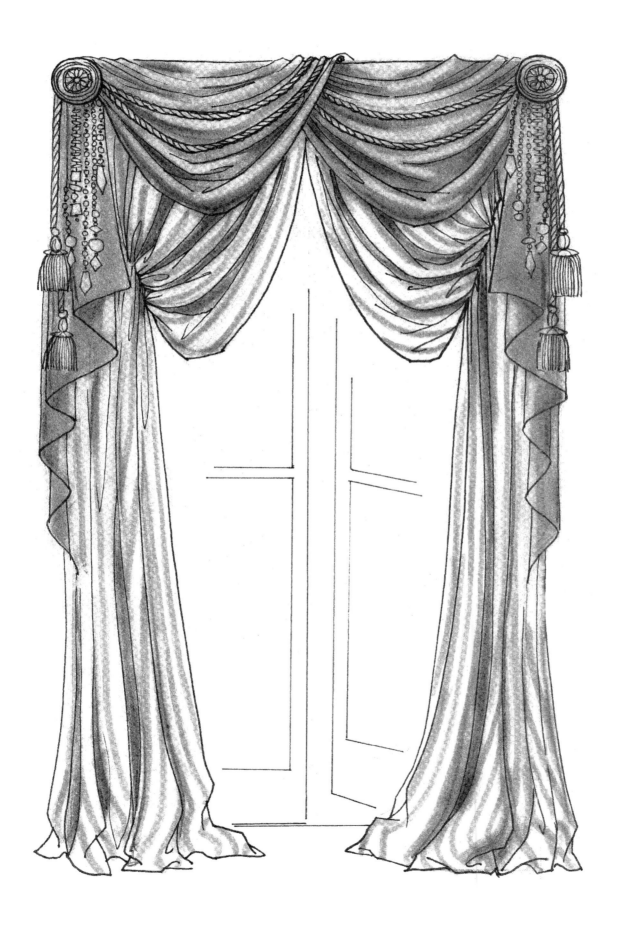

Italian stringing

dressed curtains

dressed curtains

dressed curtains

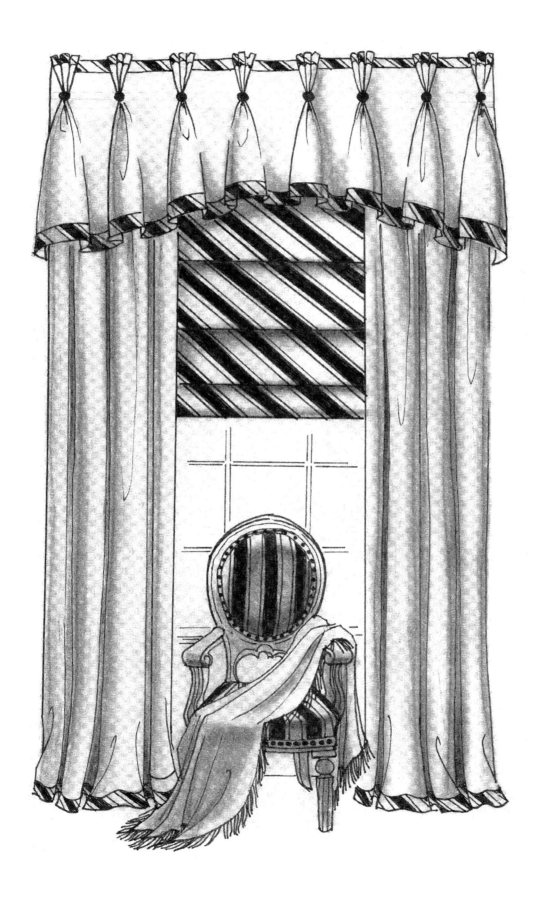

dressed curtains

dressed curtains

dressed curtains

dressed curtains

covered lathes

covered lathes

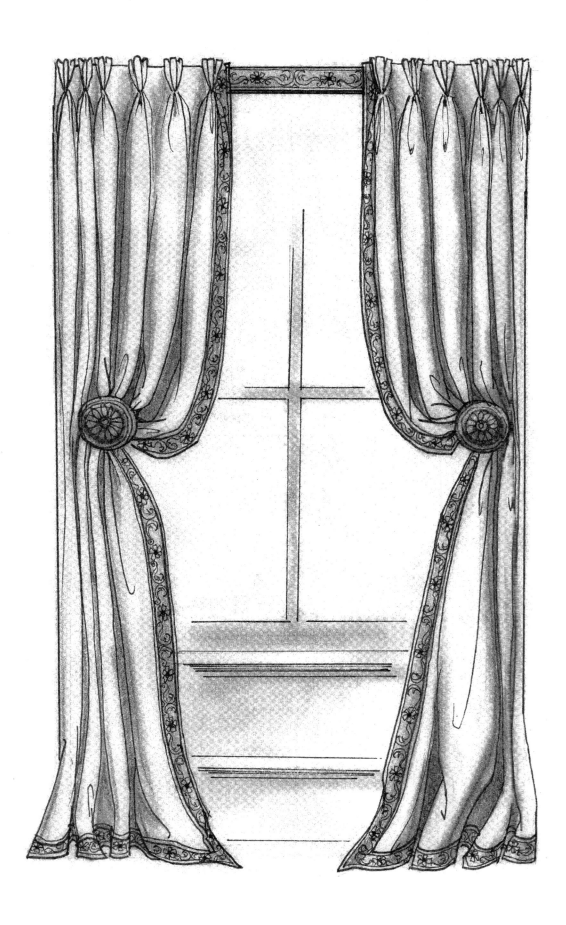

covered lathes

alcoves

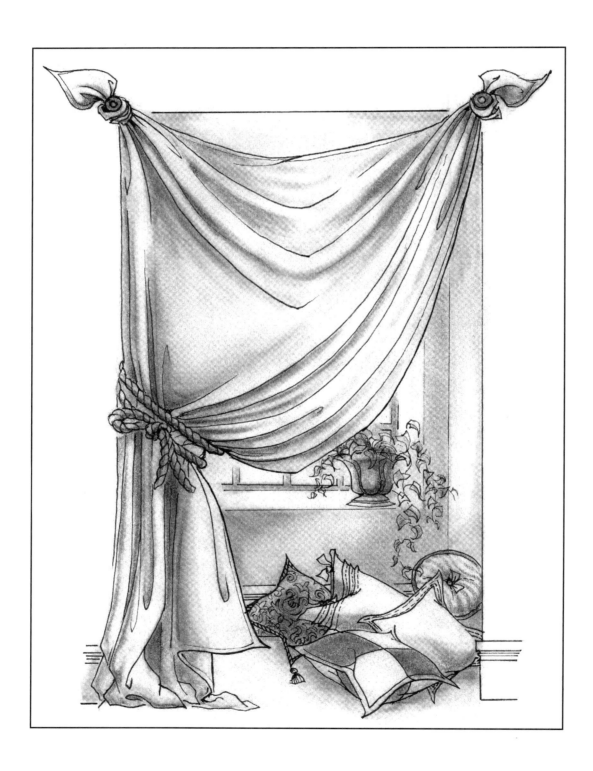

alcoves

alcoves

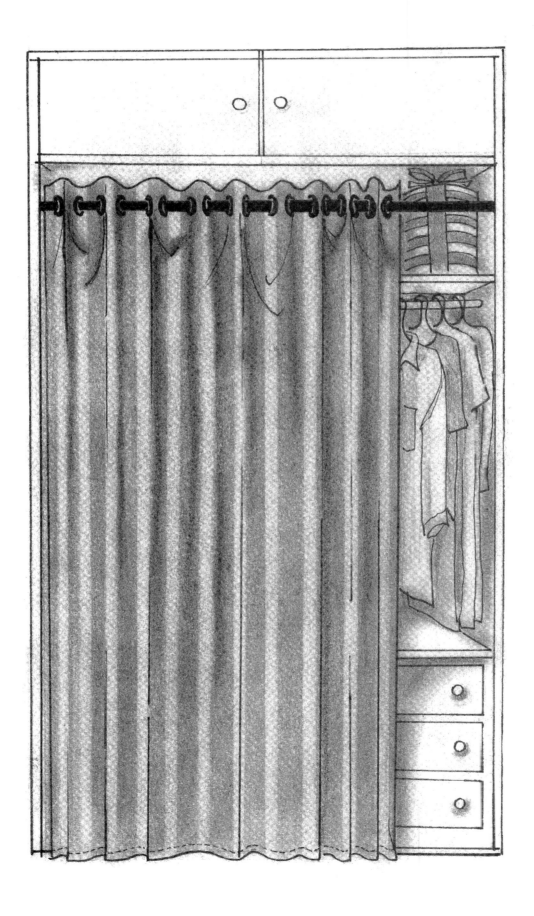

alcoves

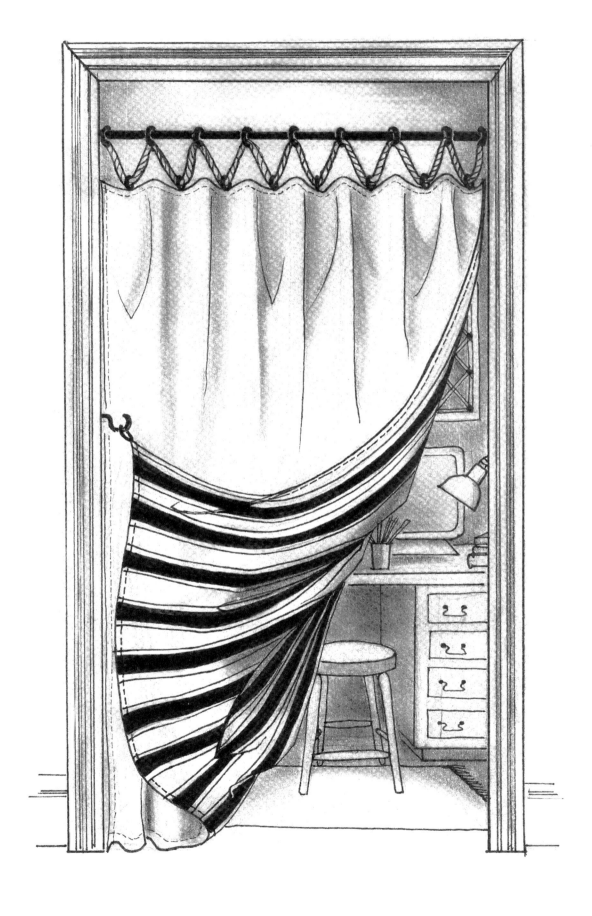

alcoves

alcoves

portières

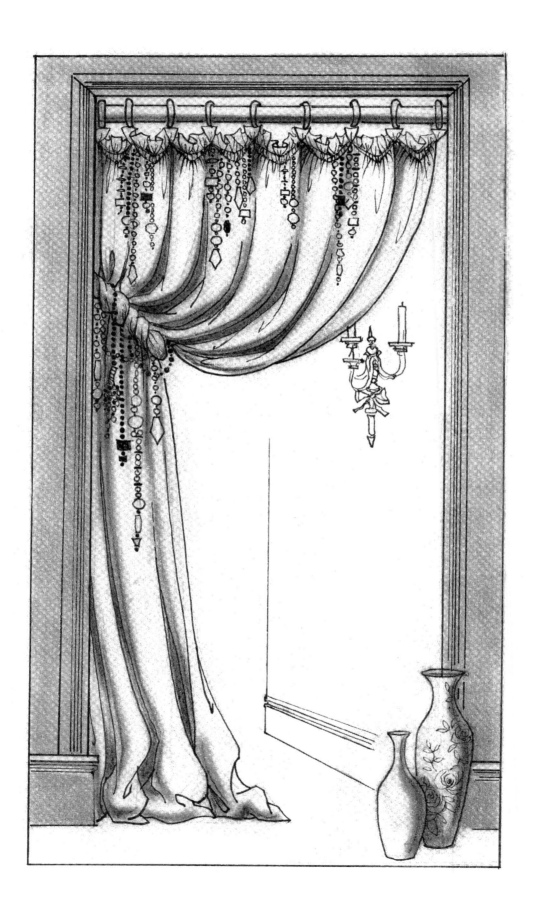

portières

portières

portières

appliquéd curtains

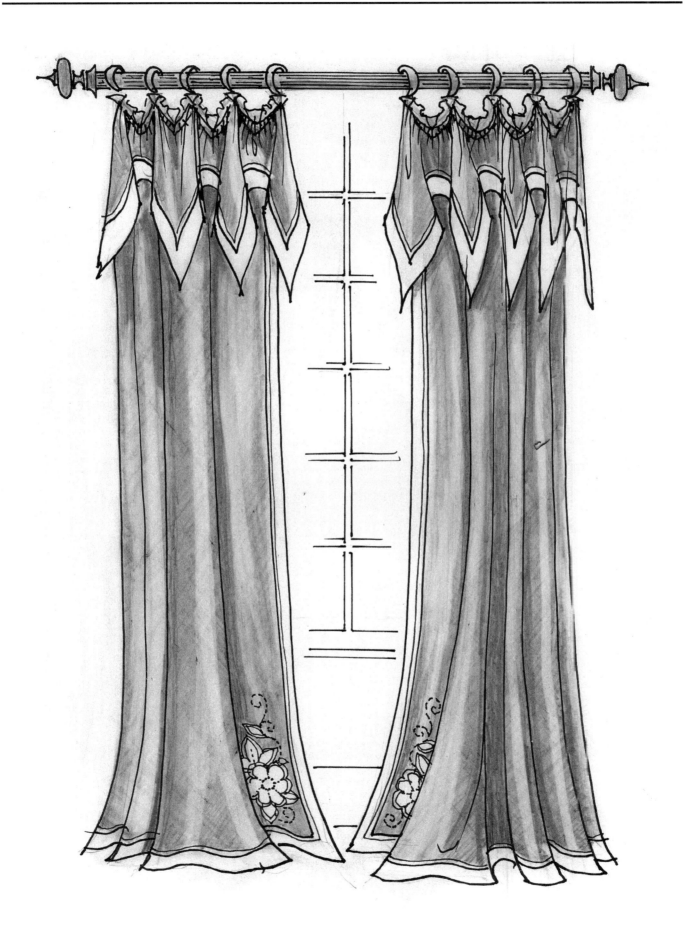

appliquéd curtains

appliquéd curtains

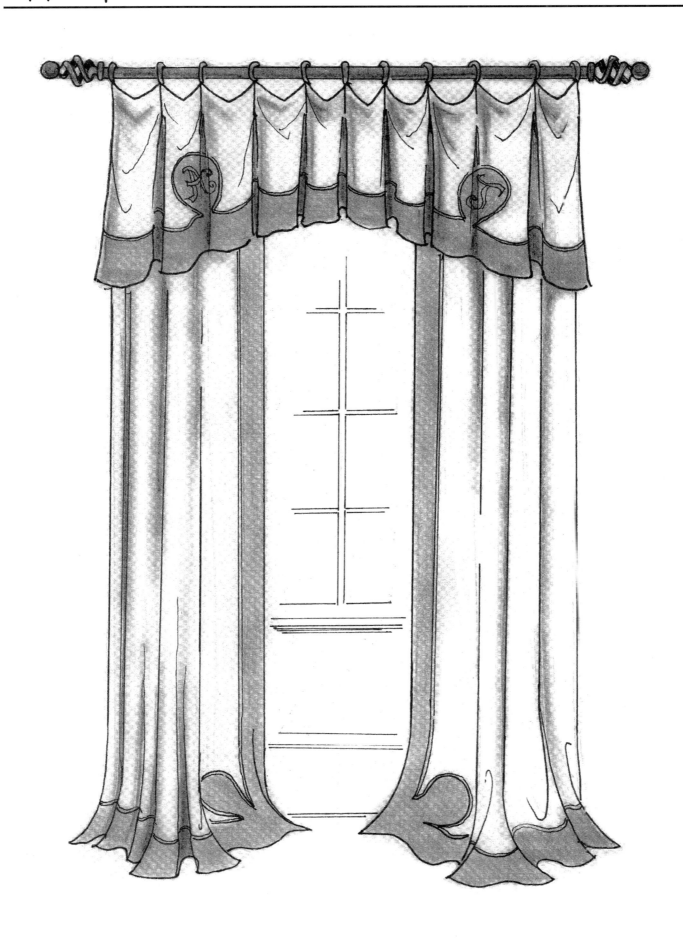

appliquéd curtains

bedroom curtains

bedroom curtains

bedroom curtains

bedroom curtains

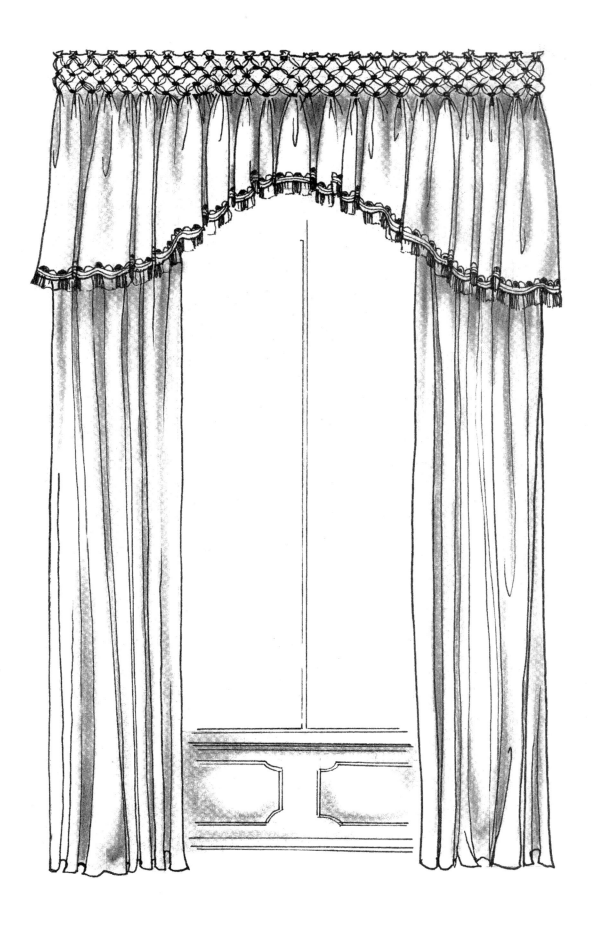

bedroom curtains

bedroom curtains

bedroom curtains

bedroom curtains

voiles/sheers

voiles/sheers

voiles/sheers

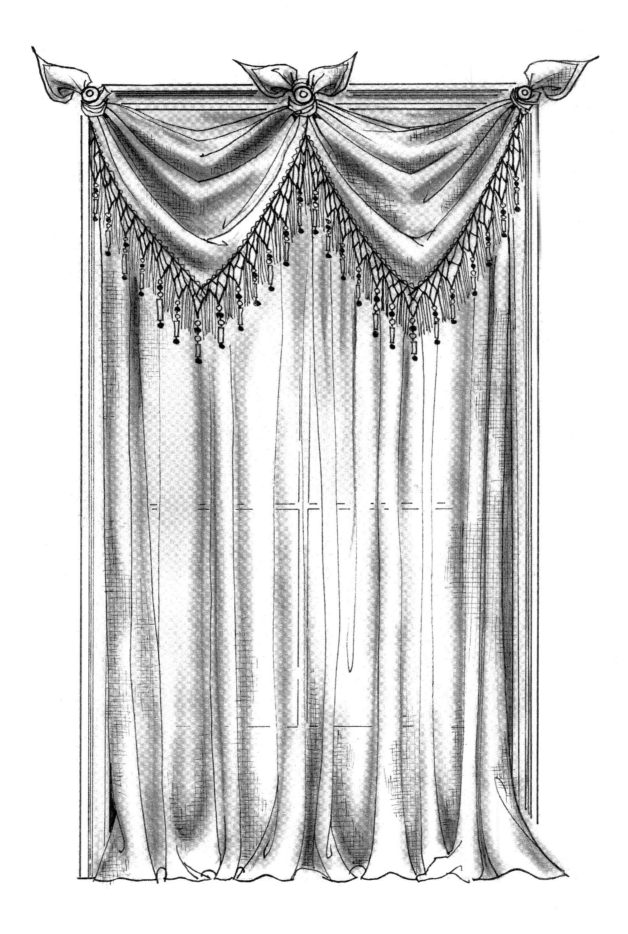

voiles/sheers

voiles/sheers

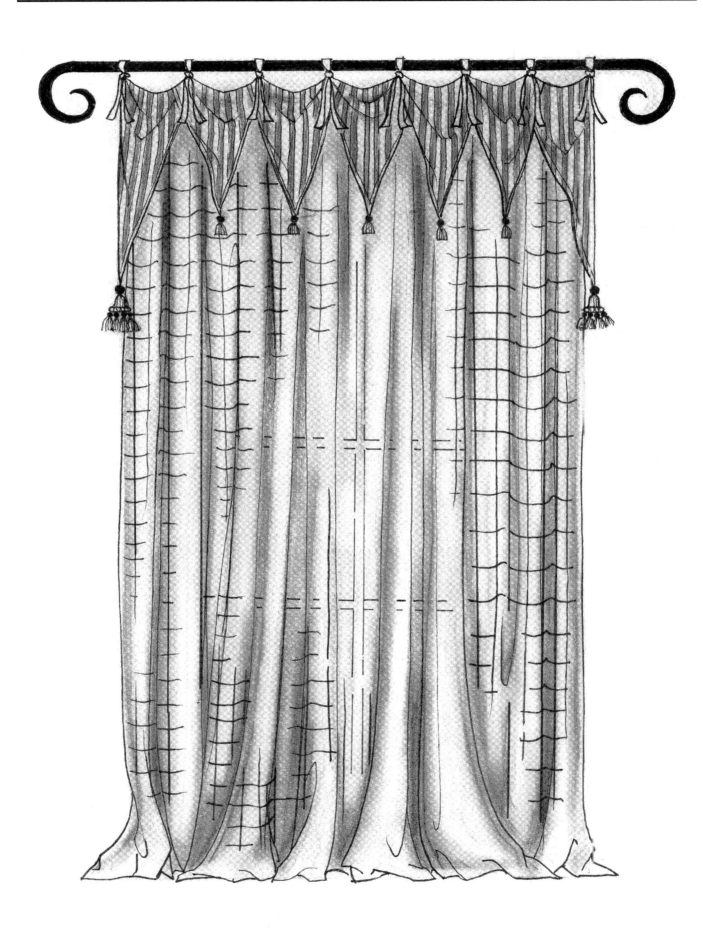

voiles/sheers

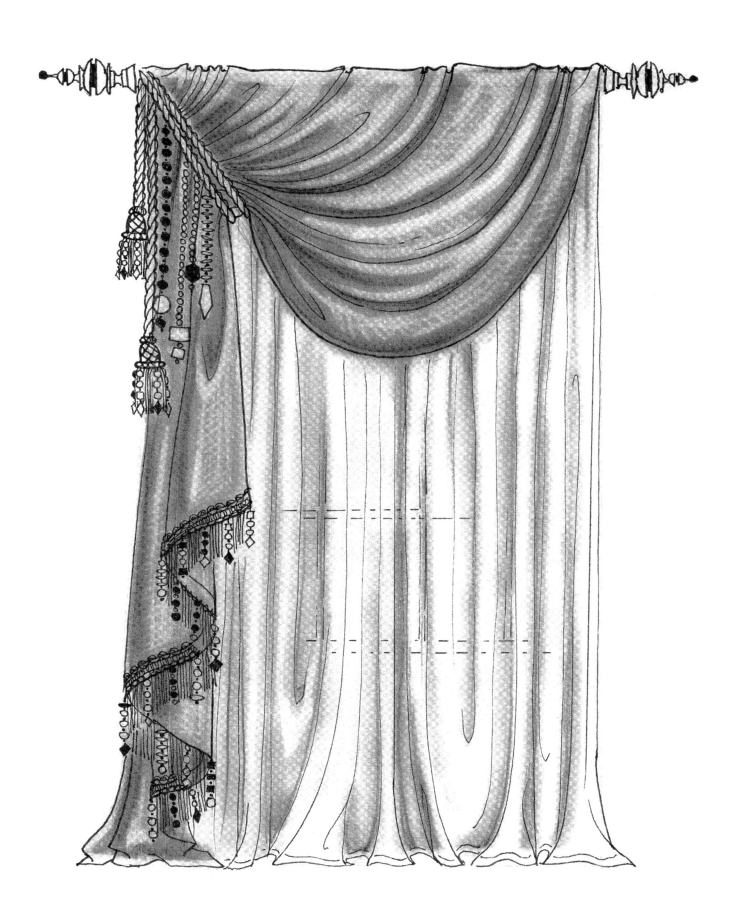

voiles/sheers

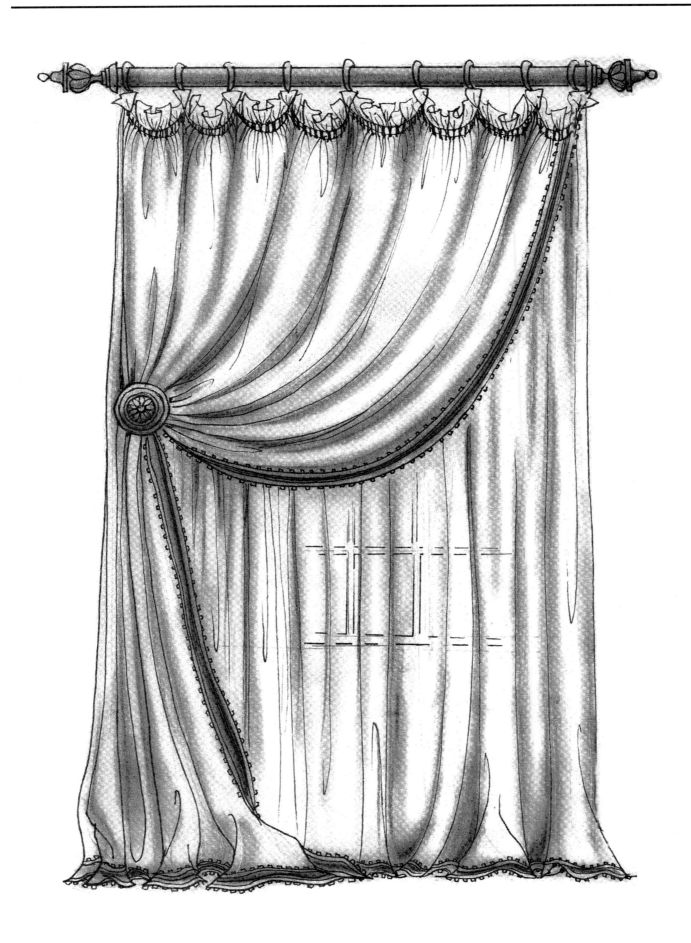

voiles/sheers

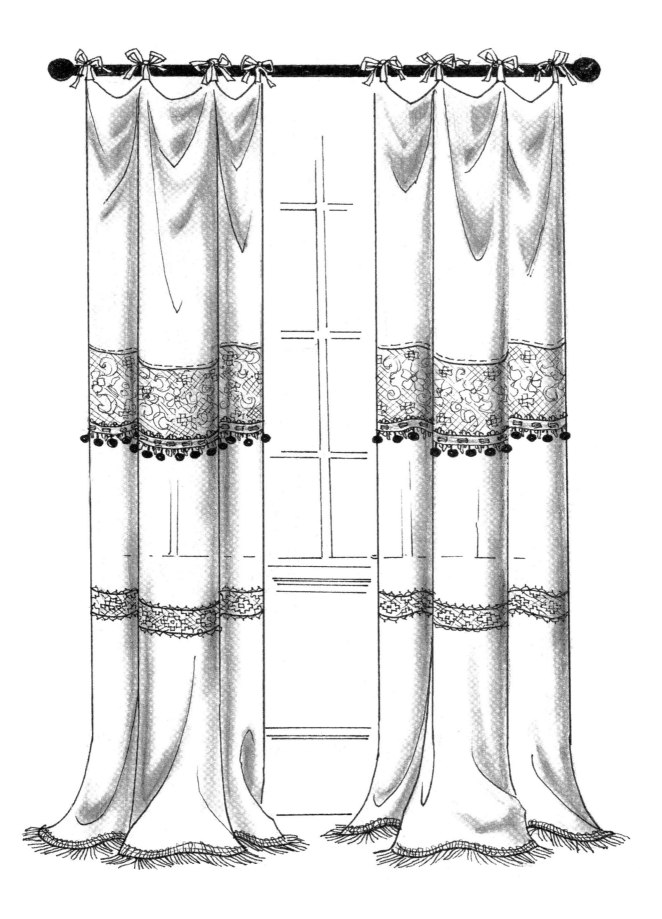

kitchen curtains/blinds

kitchen curtains/blinds

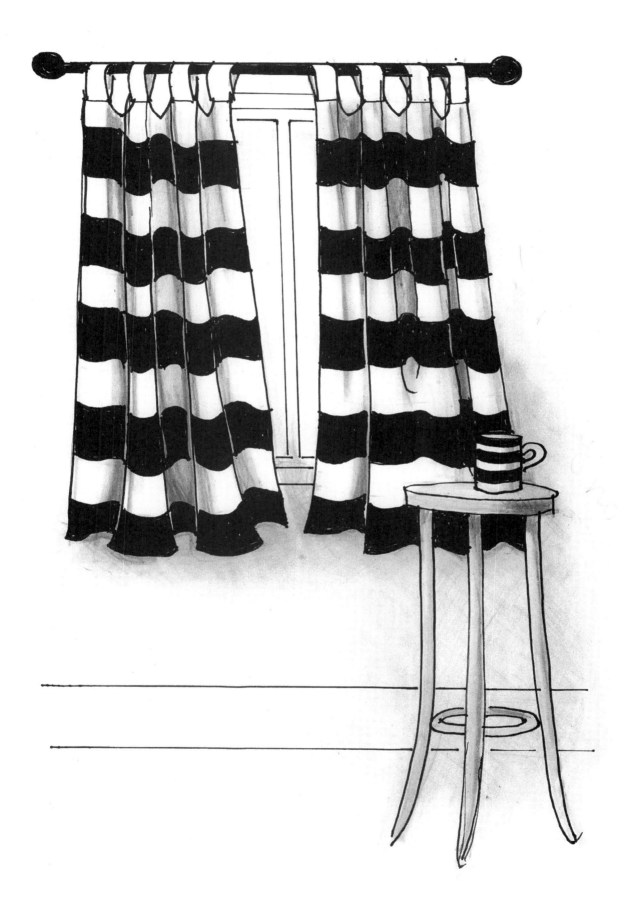

kitchen curtains/blinds

kitchen curtains/blinds

kitchen curtains/blinds

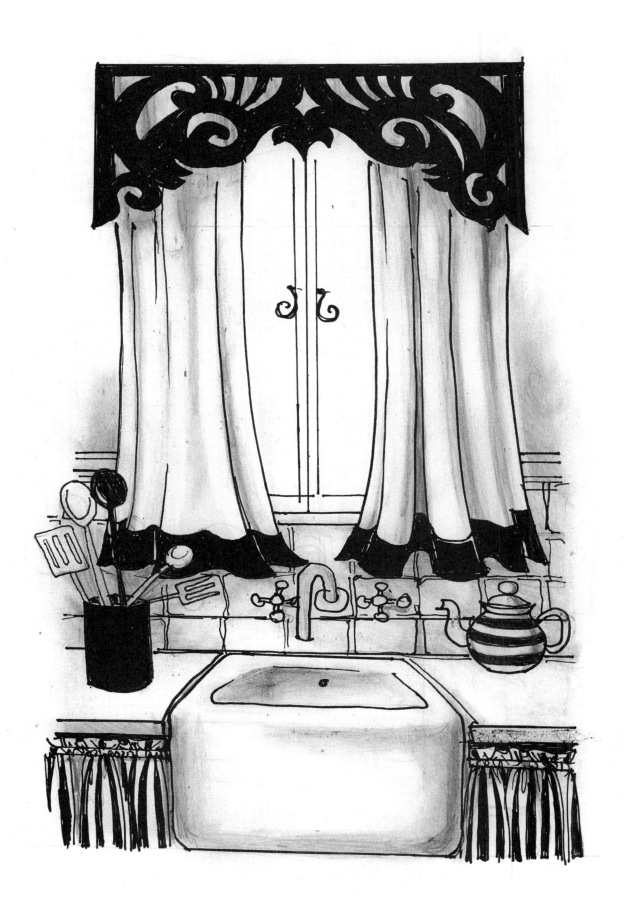

kitchen curtains/blinds

difficult windows

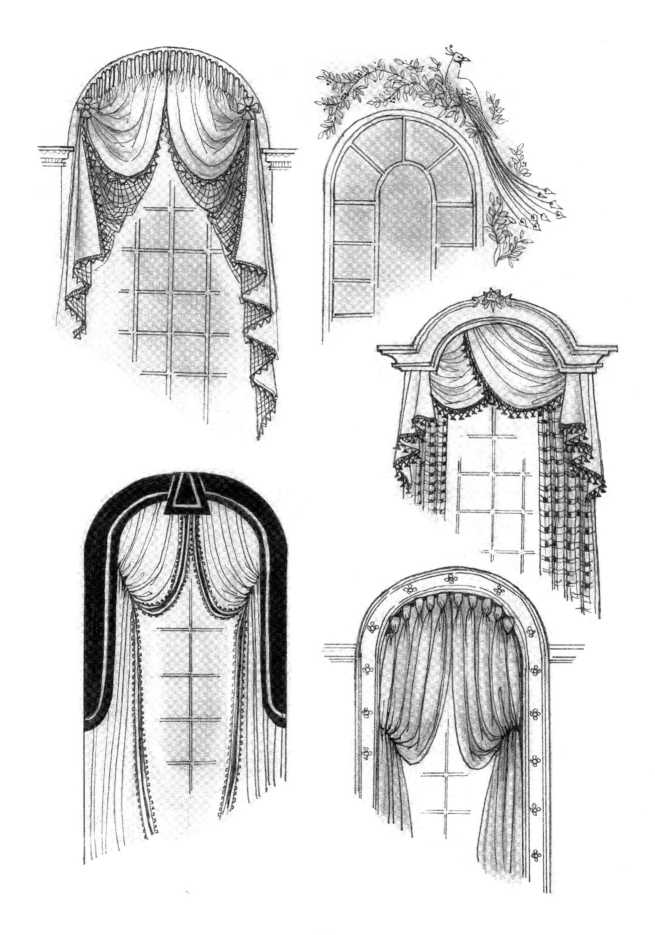

difficult windows

difficult windows

alternative window coverings

alternative window coverings

alternative window coverings

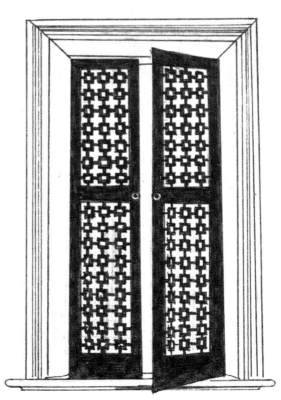

alternative window coverings

cafe/short/doors

cafe/short/doors

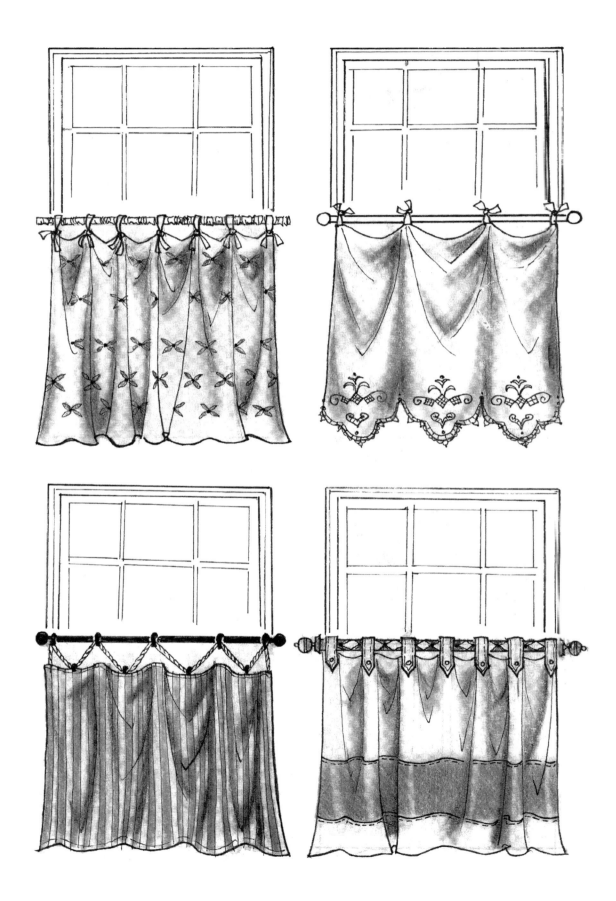

lambrequins

1

2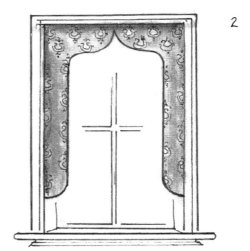

3

4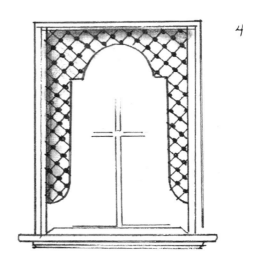

5

6

blinds/shades

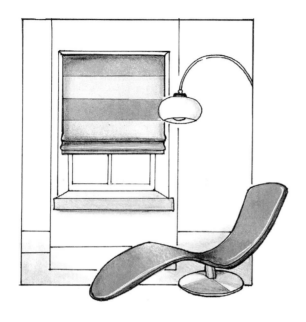

Roman

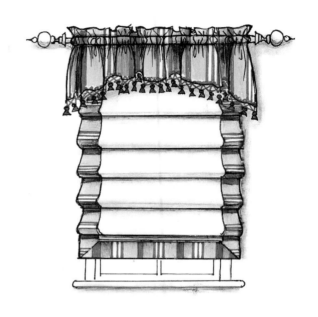

Cascade

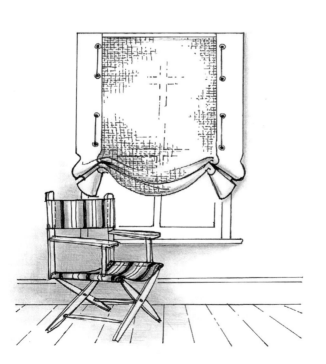

London Fold

Oriental

blinds/shades

Austrian

London Blind

Roller Blind

Roller Blind with Lambrequin

table covers

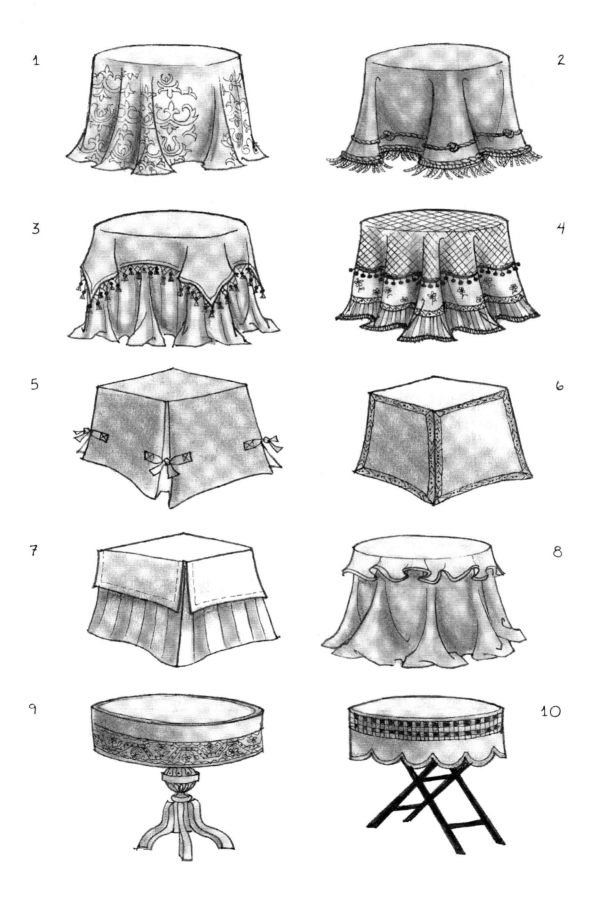

headboards

bed covers

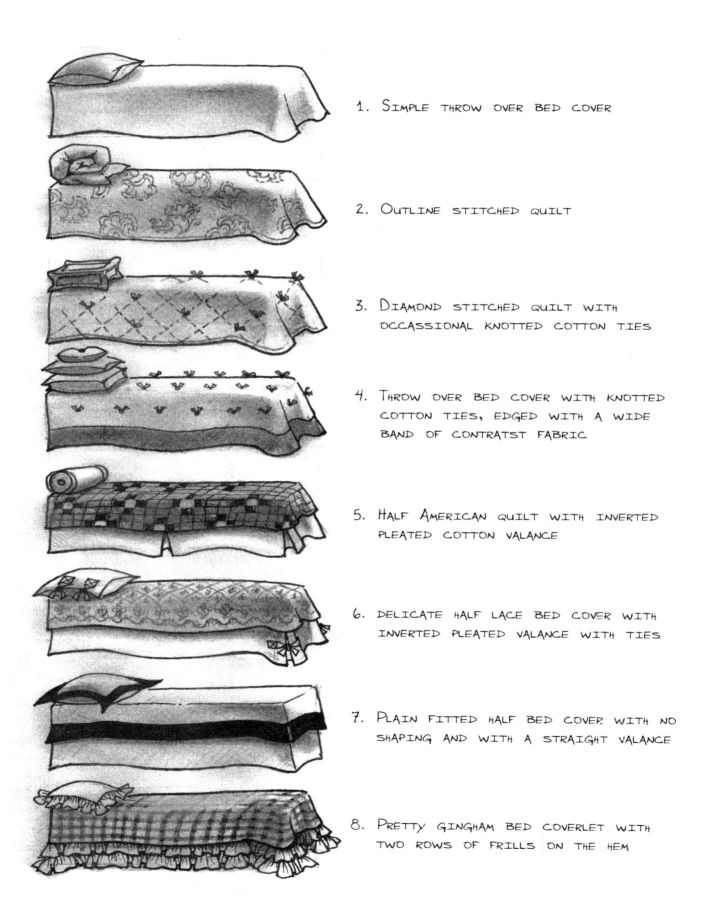

1. Simple throw over bed cover

2. Outline stitched quilt

3. Diamond stitched quilt with occassional knotted cotton ties

4. Throw over bed cover with knotted cotton ties, edged with a wide band of contratst fabric

5. Half American quilt with inverted pleated cotton valance

6. delicate half lace bed cover with inverted pleated valance with ties

7. Plain fitted half bed cover with no shaping and with a straight valance

8. Pretty gingham bed coverlet with two rows of frills on the hem

basic cushion shapes

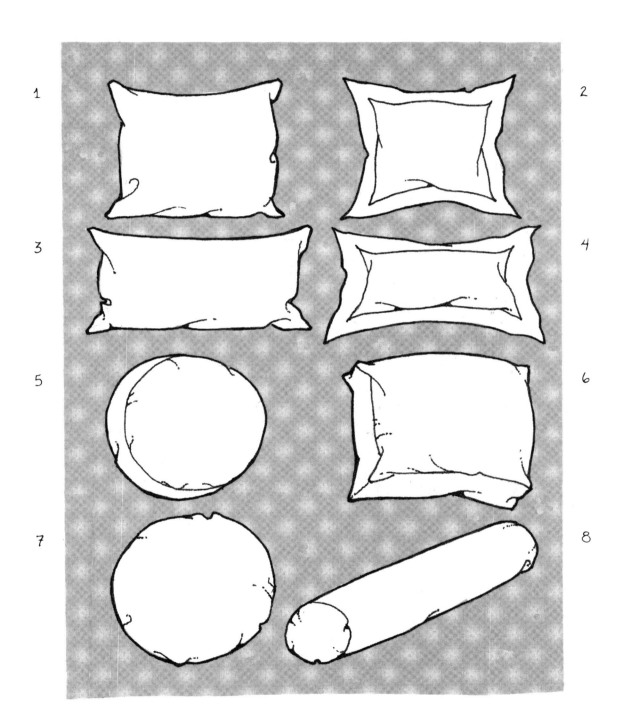

cushions